Thomas Orde, 1746–1807

AF786985

Thomas Orde, 1746–1807

Educational Innovator

Tony Lyons†

PETER LANG
Oxford - Berlin - Bruxelles - Chennai - Lausanne - New York

Bibliographic information published by the Deutsche Nationalbibliothek. The German National Library lists this publication in the German National Bibliography; detailed bibliographic data is available on the Internet at http://dnb.d-nb.de.

A catalogue record for this book is available from the British Library.

Library of Congress Cataloging-in-Publication Data

Names: Lyons, Tony, 1957- author.
Title: Thomas Orde, 1746-1807: educational innovator / Tony Lyons.
Description: Berlin; New York: Peter Lang, 2024. | Includes bibliographical references and index.
Identifiers: LCCN 2023056304 (print) | LCCN 2023056305 (ebook) | ISBN 9781803743516 (paperback) | ISBN 9781803743523 (ebook) | ISBN 9781803743530 (epub)
Subjects: LCSH: Education--Ireland--History--18th century. | Education--Ireland--History--19th century. | Education and state--Ireland--History--18th century. | Education and state--Ireland--History--19th century. | Orde, Thomas, 1746-1807.
Classification: LCC LA669.62. L963 2024 (print) | LCC LA669.62 (ebook) | DDC 370.941709/033--dc23/eng/20231229
LC record available at https://lccn.loc.gov/2023056304
LC ebook record available at https://lccn.loc.gov/2023056305

Cover image: The portrait of Order was painted by Pompeo Girolamo Batoni c.1773.
Cover design by Peter Lang Group AG

ISBN 978-1-80374-351-6 (print)
ISBN 978-1-80374-352-3 (ePDF)
ISBN 978-1-80374-353-0 (ePub)
DOI 10.3726/b21444

© 2024 Peter Lang Group AG, Lausanne
Published by Peter Lang Ltd, Oxford, United Kingdom
info@peterlang.com – www.peterlang.com

Tony Lyons has asserted his right under the Copyright, Designs and Patents Act, 1988, to be identified as Author of this Work.

All rights reserved.
All parts of this publication are protected by copyright.
Any utilisation outside the strict limits of the copyright law, without the permission of the publisher, is forbidden and liable to prosecution.
This applies in particular to reproductions, translations, microfilming, and storage and processing in electronic retrieval systems.

This publication has been peer reviewed.

Tony (Anthony) Lyons was born in Listowel, Co. Kerry on 20th April 1957 to farmers Ned Joe and Peg Lyons. He married Sadhbh De Bhulbh (Woulfe) in 1980 and they have two children Eoghan and Aisling.

Tony had suffered ill health since 2013 but this did not hinder his love of writing and as he said himself "if anything, it has fuelled my determination to keep my writing well from running dry"

Sadly, Tony passed away on 23rd February 2024 before publication of this book was finalised. He will be greatly missed by his family, friends and former colleagues and students of Mary Immaculate College, Limerick.

Contents

Acknowledgements

I would like to thank the staffs of two libraries: Mary Immaculate College Library, University of Limerick; the National Library of Ireland, Kildare Street, Dublin.

For my wife Sadhbh's patience, I owe a great debt of gratitude.

CHAPTER 1

Introduction to the Eighteenth Century: New Ideas; Orde's Background; Hely-Hutchinson

Several factors determine the development of educational systems, some of which are active at any given moment, and are contemporaneous with the system being initiated, while others, stem from the past, and have a long-lasting sway on the outcomes of various systems. It is difficult to distinguish the relevant levels of efficacy each one sustains. Each has potential persuasive powers and must be considered carefully as a possible factor in the evolution of a system. The relationship between any specific episode and the special forces will clearly determine the importance of any event as a factor. An analysis of the factors influencing developments in the history of Irish primary education must include reasonably detailed accounts of the main episodes, and a study of these is an essential preliminary to the discussion of their interaction with the unseen, persistent and inevitable forces of Irish society at any particular time. Nothing works in complete isolation from the broader world, and, so the study of the main educational developments must be fitted into the social life of the community and even into the more expansive world outlook. Thus, it is crucial to position Thomas Orde and his elaborate plan for Irish education in the 1780s within the context of historical efforts to introduce an education system and contemporary influences which may have aided or hindered further advances.

Eighteenth-century Ireland under the Georges suffered considerable neglect. The theme of many a melodious 'Aisling' or 'Vision' was that of a symbolic Ireland, a beautiful, sorrowful woman and her rightful spouse, a mythical Stuart, in the shape of 'Bonnie Prince Charlie.' The Prince was the Jacobite heir to the throne, but had little chance of ever coming to Ireland and 'saving' or 'rescuing' the country from its Protestant overlords.

The old Gaelic order of poets, bards and patronage was gone. Any hope of a Catholic revival ended in 1745 with a failed Stuart rebellion. The world of the 'file' (poet), the Brehon, the man of learning, art, poetry, whose history as an established and cultured class going back to pagan Ireland was now vanquished and all over. The Irish language was retained only by the provincial peasant classes; the Irish aristocracy were all gone, and from that viewpoint Ireland was leaderless.

In the eighteenth century, the effect of the penal laws was to confine Irish education to the pay schools. A handful of proselytizing schools had survived from the time of Henry VIII but the vast majority of the Irish people who did have some kind of formal education attended the pay schools. They were mainly Catholic in nature, but there were also Dissenter pay schools, such as Presbyterian.

The backdrop to the social aspects of Irish history during this period, and taking education as one aspect of concern for the British state in Ireland, was that a concept like education was, in reality, a micro-site of power that became colonized or adapted into the changing rationale of government and became an element in the various technologies of government aimed at managing populations. While some historians suggest the range of possible motivations for the involvement of the British state in Irish education ranged from altruism to exploitation,[1] in the context of this book the British state established a national education system in Ireland as a social technology, which aimed to create predictable patterns of behaviour on the part of the individual and the general populace.[2] Thomas Orde was a cog within that process; it was he who initiated the process, and by initiating the process the state, through subsequent inquiries merged into the field of education, and in this manner legitimized the education of the poor in Ireland as an objective of government. Orde's plan of 1787 was the first suggestion of a centralized system of education in the country and, while it was not implemented, it represented the first attempt by the state to

1 John Coolahan, *Irish Education: History and Structure* (Dublin: Institute of Public Administration, 1981), 10.

2 Mark Haugaard and Kevin Ryan, 'Power and Powerlessness', in Sara O'Sullivan, ed., *Contemporary Ireland: A Sociological Map* (Dublin: University College Press, 2007), 198.

directly intervene in educational matters, notwithstanding Tudor attempts of an earlier time. Orde's involvement in education provision in Ireland, coupled with the subsequent series of inquiries demonstrate the ongoing legitimization of education as an object of government.

Ireland, in the eighteenth century, was a country of contrasts, squalor and splendour, poverty and prosperity. The poor ate potatoes and drank cheap whisky. Rioting was the result of food shortages. The famine of 1739 was a greater disaster proportionately than the famine of the 1840s. The landlord estate system of agrarian management meant that landowners were often the principal local decision-makers, and in contrast the Georgian period was one of wealth for landowners. They owned country mansions and town houses.

Roads, railways and canals were being built. Ireland only experienced the fringes of the Industrial Revolution, bar the north-eastern part of the island. These roads, railways and canals offered little by way of improvement to the circumstances of the general population. The pockets of the gentry and propertied classes were lined during the eighteenth century. Little wonder then that education was used at the end of the century and during the next as an agent in maintaining the status quo. The political, social and economic supremacy of a small but leading class was preserved. The growing attachment to things mechanical, technical and scientific throughout the eighteenth century is evidence of the ruling classes, the business people, viewing education as a tool, as a political and economic football with which to preserve and advance their own ends.

As the century wore on the Penal Laws were relaxed, and in the 1780s and 1790s repealed. Ascendancy and middle-class Ireland functioned mainly within the confines of the old Pale, with Dublin as its centre of power, and the city itself gaining in status within the Empire to become its second city. At the end of this century, the powers that be took it upon themselves an interest in educational matters.

Eighteenth-century Ireland, in the words of Lecky, was both ambivalent and inspirational. The likes of W. B. Yeats and Elizabeth Bowen imagined the era in the following terms:

> The great bold rooms, the high doors imposed an order on life. Sun blazed in at the windows, fires roared in the grates. There was a sweet, fresh-planed smell from the

> floors. Life still kept a touch of colonial vigour; at the same time, because of the glory of everything, it was bound up in the quality of a dream.[3]

The values expressed above meant nothing to the Catholic or Dissenting tradition, as they were very much associated with those of English heritage, the Protestant (Anglican) religion, and in Ireland in the eighteenth century, the Ascendancy class. From 1704 onwards diversification of classes (at least two) was rife; those who subscribed to Anglicanism ruled the roost, while those who were beyond the castle walls should be happy with the crumbs. A Catholic or a Dissenter[4] could not aspire towards parliament; nor could he become an officer in the army; education, too, was curtailed, both at home and abroad. From 1704 all members of the Irish Parliament had to be members of the Church of Ireland. This legislative underwriting excluded Catholics and Presbyterians. As a result, many Presbyterians left Ireland for North America during the eighteenth century.

The Catholic and some of the Dissenter population devised their own illegal type of schooling, namely, the Hedge Schools, or more accurately Pay Schools. In tandem with their social class these schools were also beyond the Pale; they were without any state sponsorship, and the community paid for their child's education. These were private institutions, paid for by the slightly better off poor– the rest did not have the wherewithal to participate. Yes, Ireland was a nation of at least two parts, the one in power being the minority, and the rest victimized for being what they were. It was a two-tier state of privilege on the one hand and not much more than piety on the other.

The Enlightenment lapped round Irish public life in the last two decades of the eighteenth century, before receding. There were two great waves of hope and confidence, which in different ways inspired succeeding

3 Quoted in R. F. Foster, *Modern Ireland, 1600–1972* (London: Penguin Books, 1989), 168.

4 Being a Dissenter meant refusal to accept an established doctrine, and in this particular instance, not accepting the tenets of the Established Church (Anglican/ Church of Ireland). Refusing to accept one doctrine implies the existence of another.

generations. The Volunteers, the Dungannon Convention, and the Declaration of Legislative Independence of the Irish parliament in 1782,[5] together with the reform of some of the worst of the Penal Laws and commercial restrictions, represented the first wave, influenced by America. When that wave was checked, another more radical wave inspired by France, which sought reform but culminated in revolution, followed.[6]

The eighteenth century brought with it new ideas. It was an era of change: the steam engine brought new lifeblood to many walks of life in many countries. Writers, such as Tom Paine, introduced the seedlings that would mature into philosophical treatises on government reform; Mary Wollstonecraft was determined to pave the way for an improved rite of passage for womankind; the 'enthronement' of reason led to the temporary overthrow of authority in the traditional association with religion; individual rights were now being asserted, to such an extent that it was possible and accepted, that the individual can think for himself.

From a practical viewpoint the printed word surged ahead and gained currency in the eighteenth century. Prior to this period, printed books were the preserve of the elite, and wealthy, but in the late eighteenth century they became available to the majority of the people. In the absence of statistics on literacy and reading during this period, we have to try to gauge from later figures the extent of reading ability. In 1841 almost half of the population over 5 years of age was able to read, but there were regional variations. In parts of Ulster, 85–90 per cent could read, while in parts of Connacht, it was as low as 10–15 per cent. 'By projecting backwards from the 1841 data, using age cohort figures, it has been estimated that literacy in the later eighteenth century had already reached 55 per cent among men

5 This left the connection between the two kingdoms dangerously vague and imprecise. In 1785 Britain made an attempt to make the connection tighter and better-defined, but the attempt failed amid much bitterness on both sides of the Irish sea. Then, in 1788, King George III went mad, and it became necessary to appoint a Regent to rule the two kingdoms while his insanity lasted. The king recovered, but the episode served to increase the desire of British politicians to draw the two kingdoms more closely together, if necessary by a Union.

6 Martin Mansergh, *The Legacy of History* (Cork: Mercier Press, 2003).

and 34 per cent for women.'[7] These figures reveal that Ireland lagged behind England where male and female literacy rates stood at 60 per cent and 40 per cent respectively. One must not ignore the fact that many people in Ireland spoke the vernacular and English was still a foreign language to many. By 1800, English had become the 'language of fair and market' but we can only say that about those people living east of the line from Derry in the north and Cork in the south. Those on the west of that line still spoke Irish in their everyday affairs.[8]

Literacy can be judged by a multi-faceted level of criteria: from the person who can write his name, to the person to has a well-thumbed bible, to the cultivated person who is familiar with a range of literary publications. It was common knowledge in the late eighteenth century that the lower classes received their literary prowess from reading 'chap' books, with their stories of robbers, dexterous thieves and pirates, and chivalrous romances, and also, useful stories of voyages, travels and history.[9]

Considerable confessional allegiance was a major factor in the increase in literacy levels in the eighteenth century. Ireland was not alone in this: the Dutch Republic, the Scottish lowlands and Sweden were areas of Protestant dominance in which the Bible was the main source of literary prowess. Allied to that was the effect that the pay schools had on literacy levels on the peasantry as by 1800, 400,000 were attending these schools, most of them Catholic.[10]

The expansion of print was closely linked to urbanization and to the growing communications network that accompanied it.[11] It was not just the existence of bookshops and coffee-houses that mattered, but the critical mass of lawyers, doctors, teachers, traders and printers living in towns, all of whom required the ability to read and write so as to advance their careers.

7 Figures taken from Niall Ó Ciosáin, *Print and Popular Culture in Ireland, 1750–1850* (Basingstoke, 1997), 38. Cited in Ian McBride, *Eighteenth-Century Ireland: The Isles of Slaves* (Dublin: Gill and Macmillan, 2009), 56–57.

8 See Ian McBride, *Eighteenth-Century Ireland,* 59–61.

9 Whitley Stokes, *Projects for Re-establishing the Internal Peace and Tranquillity of Ireland* (Dublin, 1799), 41. Cited in Ian McBride, *Eighteenth-Century Ireland,* 57.

10 Ian McBride, *Eighteenth-Century Ireland,* 58.

11 Ian McBride, *Eighteenth-Century Ireland,* 59.

With the failure of this new social order in the wake of the post-revolutionary period in places like France, human reason alone proved to be insufficient. Consequently, reaction set in, in all fields of human activity, not least in education. Somewhere in the midst of all this was the ideal of human freedom, and this was not forgotten.

In educational terms, this ideal of freedom was expressed in many fashions. The Edgeworths, Richard Lovell and his daughter Maria, contributed in no mean way to the dialogue in educational discourse. Their image of education should not be to teach children reading, grammar, or Latin, or arithmetic ... but gradually to give them the desire to learn ...[12] R. L. Edgeworth did not scold one of his children when the latter broke one of his toys, but, instead he encouraged him to repeat the action on a different toy. For Edgeworth, this was a trail of discovery, and it should not be truncated.

The innovative education plan by Thomas Orde paved the way for subsequent investigations as well as bringing the day closer when Ireland would have a national system of education. His plan set in train a significant number of events involving government participation in education provision in Ireland.

Orde's Background

Thomas Orde 1746–1807, 1st Baron Bolton was born into a well-respected family of East Orde and Morpeth, Northumberland. In 1772 he travelled in France and Switzerland, and in 1774 in Flanders, Holland and Germany. He was appointed to the two Duchy of Lancaster offices under the chancellorship of Lord Hyde, later Earl of Clarendon. However, information about Orde before he entered parliament is scant.

Having acquired a parliamentary seat for Aylesbury, there is no direct evidence how Orde achieved this. On 10 December 1779, John Robinson

12 R. L. Edgeworth, *Essays on Professional Education* (London: Johnston and Co, 1809), 40–41. Republished Cambridge University Press, 2013.

wrote to Lord Sandwich[13] that at Aylesbury he could put Sandwich's friend Lord Chesterfield 'in a way to bring in a Member of his own very easily'; and though Orde was not Chesterfield's first choice, on 7 September, the day of the poll, he was described by an Aylesbury elector as 'thought a man qualified by Earl Chesterfield'.[14]

He later entered parliament for Harwich (1784–1796). He served as Secretary to the Treasury (1782–1783) and as Chief Secretary for Ireland (1784–1787). In 1782, he was appointed to the Privy Council of Ireland.[15]

Orde was an unlikely candidate for the role of education reformer when it meant the occurrence of verbal pugilistic outbursts in the Irish House of Commons. He had gained administrative experience in Whitehall, though for limited periods of time. On his appointment as Irish Chief Secretary he proved to be an able administrator. Kelly, however, feels that 'he was neither outgoing nor extroverted and was plainly ill at ease with the convivial niceties and public performances that were so integral a part of the chief secretary's duties'.[16] Orde was probably more at ease when out of the limelight, and more effective as a result. Generally speaking, documents and paper work appealed to the Chief Secretary, but he was at sea when it came to managing people. Orde has been described as 'an amusing person and obviously a great character',[17] 'the man on the spot' and at the other extreme as 'a cold, cautious, slow and sententious man, tolerably well informed but not very talented with a mind neither powerful nor feeble'.[18] In the footnotes in '*The Complete Peerage*' we find the following ditty:

13 L. Namier, ed., *The History of Parliament: The House of Commons 1754–1790*, Thomas Orde.

14 Namier, *The History of Parliament,* Thomas Orde.

15 Thomas Orde (1746–1807). History of Parliament Online. Historyofparliamentonline.org.

16 James Kelly, 'The Context and Course of Thomas Orde's Plan of Education of 1787', *The Irish Journal of Education* XX/1 (1986), 3–26.

17 Right Hon. R. W. A. Orde-Powlett, 7th Baron Bolton, in a letter to Colm McElroy, 26 February 1993. McElroy duly note in the footnote that this assessment many have been tainted and should be view with caution as the letter-writer is a relative of Thomas Orde. See McElroy, C. *Thomas Orde, 1746–1807 ...,* 11, fn.

18 Sir Jonah Barrington, *Decline and Fall of the Irish Nation* (New York: P. J. Kenedy, 1896), 50–57.

He is thus satirized in the Rolliad:[19]
Tall and erect, unmeaning, mute and pale,
O'er a blank face no gleams of thought prevail.[20]

As is the case with many personages of note, the truth lies somewhere in the middle. Clearly, some individuals did not approve of Orde. Lord Mornington[21] writing in June 1784 to the Earl of Charlemont, who had asked him to intercede on his (Charlemont's) behalf on a certain matter with Orde, had this to say:

> You are now desirous that I should quicken the progress of such measures ... by application to Orde. Now, my dear Lord ... I must frankly confess to you that I have found so much reason to distrust Mr. Orde in every respect, both public and private, that I do not chuse [sic] to communicate with him where I can possibly avoid it .... I certainly never will submit to the influence of a secondary and inferior person.[22]

The provost of Trinity College, Dublin also had some misgivings about the Chief Secretary. With the death of the Duke of Rutland, who sponsored Orde for the role of Chief Secretary, Orde's star began to wane somewhat, and he was replaced by Alleyne Fitzherbert (October 1787). Speaking of Fitzherbert, Hely-Hutchinson, the Provost of the University of Dublin remarked:

> He is a real man of business, with that degree of accuracy and precision which a clear understanding acquires by long habits of business. He knows when to be silent, a science in which our friend Orde has taken no degree at Cambridge.[23]

19 Rolliad: A work of British satire, directed at William Pitt, the Younger.

20 *The Complete Peerage,* vol. 2, Oakham to Richmond (London, 1912), 216. Republished G. E. Cokayne, *The Complete Peerage,* vol. 2 (London: Franklin Classics, 2018).

21 Born Richard Colley, elevated to the Irish Peerage as Baron Mornington, and Lord Lieutenant of Ireland on two occasions.

22 H.M.C. Mss. Of Earl of Charlemont, 1–2. Thirteenth Report, Appendix, pt. VIII. *The Manuscripts and Correspondence of James, First Earl of Charlemont,* vol. 2, 1784–1799, pt. 4, (1894). See McElroy's Thesis, p. 12.

23 H. M. C. *Twelfth Report, Appendix, pt. IX: Manuscripts of the Duke of Beaufort, K. G. the Earl of Donoughmore, and Others*, p. 416 (1890–1891). Interestingly, Fitzherbert was described by Forbes in a letter to Grattan as a manic depressive in the last stages

On a particular occasion Rutland described Orde as 'indefatigable and a most able and valuable servant to his Majesty'.[24] It is apparent that the Lord Lieutenant came to depend upon the Chief Secretary quite a lot, especially regarding the latter's organizational and managerial skills. Historians, though, have differed on the interpretation of Orde's skills and qualities; some are in favour of Orde, while others decry him. According to the various interpretations Orde had a wide-ranging distribution of aptitudes and political potency. In such a manner, he is depicted as being 'able and conciliatory' and also as possessing 'lack of drive'.[25] Perhaps, we should grant Prime Minister Pitt one final word on Orde's character and abilities, when, following the collapse of the Commercial Bill, 'he had been personally impressed by Orde's devotion to his work, and he signalled his confidence in him by nominating him to the British privy council shortly afterwards.'[26] The Irish staring-point for a revised commercial arrangement between the two countries had begun at the end the 'stormy' 1784 parliamentary session calling for 'a wise and well digested plan for a liberal arrangement of commercial intercourse between Great Britain and Ireland',[27] which Orde accepted, with alterations.

Pitt himself was able to give Orde a convincing account of the British government's success in resisting amendments designed to remould the commercial provisions to Ireland's disadvantage.[28] He took the line that the best way to counter the argument that Britain was conferring too many

---

of cirrhosis who, moreover, was 'totally ignorant of the business of Parliament, and the internal concerns of these kingdoms'. Cited in G. O'Brien, *Anglo-Irish Politics in the Age of Grattan and Pitt* (Dublin: Irish Academic Press, 1987).

24 H.M.C. *Mss. Of the Duke of Rutland, Report 14, Appendix 1–2,* vol. III, p. 150 (1894–1896). On another occasion he wrote of Orde to Sydney, 'I cannot adequately express his unwearied exertions and prudent management.'

25 Both quotations in C. McElroy, *Thomas Orde, 1746–1807,* 13.

26 J. Kelly, *Prelude to Union: Anglo-Irish Politics in the 1780s* (Cork: Cork University Press, 1992), 217. In footnote 21, p. 217 Kelly draws attention to Pitt's opinion of Orde four years later when it was 'much less favourable'.

27 *Irish Parliamentary Register,* ii, 217.

28 Pitt to Rutland, Putney Heath, 21 May 1785, *Correspondence between the Right Honble; William Pitt and Charles Duke of Rutland, Lord Lieutenant of Ireland, Forgotten Books,* 102–103.

commercial benefits on Ireland, was by tightening the stipulations whereby Ireland was riveted into place in the imperial scheme of things.[29]

Contemporary Views on Orde

Both Orde and Rutland took up their respective postings in Ireland in the same year, 1784, and it appears that each complemented the other. The Duke was an MP for the University of Cambridge, and a supporter of Pitt, and as Pitt was promoted to the Premiership, Rutland became Lord Privy Seal, before being transferred to Ireland as Lord Lieutenant.[30] During his time in Ireland, he developed a reputation as a hell-raiser, which aroused the wrath of many, 'but this was compensated for by his conviviality … which gave the viceroyalty a style manifestly absent during the incumbencies of his predecessors'.[31] A great many doubts were expressed regarding the unsuitability of the Duke of Rutland for the onerous task of Lord Lieutenant of Ireland. One observation was that 'if there is one man upon earth more unfit for that situation than another, it is his Grace'.[32]

Rutland was very much aware of Lord Mornington's far-reaching criticisms of Orde, to the extent that he took it upon himself to defend

29 Pitt to Orde, 29 May 1785; See Malcomson, A. P. W., *John Foster: The Politics of the Anglo-Irish Ascendancy* (Oxford: Oxford University Press, 1978), 54.

30 Direct representative of the monarch; head of the Irish executive government; other versions of title: Judiciar; Lord Deputy to the seventeenth century; Viceroy (deputy king). As head of government he presided over the Chief Secretary, the Under-Secretary, and three Lord Justices (the Lord Chancellor of Ireland; the Speaker of the Irish House of Commons; the Church of Ireland primate of All Ireland). His headquarters were in Dublin Castle, but in 1781 moved to the Viceregal Lodge (Árus an Uachtaráin) in the Phoenix Park.

31 J. Kelly, *Prelude to Union, Anglo-Irish Politics in the 1780s* (Cork: Cork University Press, 1992).

32 Sir G. Ross, ed., *The Correspondence of Charles, First Marquess Cornwallis*, vol. 1 (London: J. Murray, 1859), 160. See Kelly, *Prelude to Union …*, 77. However, Kelly resurrects Rutland and elevates him to a respectable *savoir faire* later on the same page.

his Chief Secretary to the Prime Minister. Rutland's brief period in Ireland allowed him ample opportunity to applaud Orde when communicating with Pitt. Thus, as early as 1785 he wrote:

> It would be [an] injustice to mention Mr. Orde's name without expressing my satisfaction of his labours and endeavours to reconcile men's minds to the various difficulties which have arisen. I must bear the amplest testimony to his indefatigable zeal and exertions.[33]

On other occasions, Rutland, described Orde's sense of application to his role in Ireland as 'diligent and conscientious'. He also maintained that the Chief Secretary's conduct had never been distinguished by any inclination towards objects of emoluments 'nor has he shown any aspiration after rewards except those which have resulted from the consciousness of his own mind, and which are the honest gain of every worthy man's ambition'.[34]

It would appear that the appointment of Orde to the position of Chief Secretary for Ireland complemented Rutland's position as Lord Lieutenant. An examination of the letters, accounts, plans and so on reveals that Rutland looked upon Orde as a man who could be of enormous asset, as a man of the greatest industry and diligence, a determined man who had few equals in terms of sheer application.[35]

Orde's health was of great concern during his tenure of office in Ireland. 'It is very difficult to establish precisely what his complaint was as his symptoms varied from time to time.'[36] James Kelly attests to the fact that, at least, Orde's eye infection obliged him to resort to an amanuensis.[37]

33 Quoted in C. McElroy, *Thomas Orde 1746–1807: Educational Innovator ...*, 12–13.

34 H.M.C. Mss. Of the Duke of Rutland, Report 14, Appendix 1–2, vol. III, August 1787, p. 100.

35 Sir G. Ross, ed., *The Correspondence of Charles, the First Marquis Cornwallis,* vol. 1, 77–78. James Kelly states that Orde 'was quite capable of managing the Irish parliament' J. Kelly, *Prelude to Union, Anglo-Irish Politics in the 1780s* (Cork: Cork University Press, 1992).

36 C. McElroy, *Thomas Orde, 1746–1807: Educational Innovator ...*, *14*.

37 Orde to Sydney, 14 April, 1785 (B.P., MS 16359, f. 14); Cited in James Kelly, *Prelude to Union: Anglo-Irish Politics in the 1780s* (Cork: Cork University Press, 1992), 129. Amanuensis: a person employed to take dictation or copy a manuscript. ...' and

Perhaps, the Chief Secretary suffered from a version of hypochondria as his correspondence during his three years in Ireland contains many references to his poor health. When opening a letter and responding to its contents he usually began by apologizing for not writing earlier. This failure would be laid at the state of his health and would also include a brief account of his current condition. And, as Colm McElroy points out, Orde was very open when writing to his 'friend' the Duke of Rutland, especially when it came to the state of his health. As early as the middle of 1785, he was apologizing 'for employing an amanuensis on account of the state of my health and particularly of my eyes'.[38]

However, though his health may have been poorly, he still managed to write his plans for a police force for Dublin and his plans for an education system for Ireland, all during the dead of Winter 1786, and, of course, he was heavily involved in the negotiations surrounding the Commercial Bill. Again, writing to Rutland he exclaimed that 'I have been rather hurried for some days, and my foolish nerves are put into awkward agitation by it'.[39] The violence was often very savage, with tarring and smearing, stripping and covering the tar with goose down.[40] While reporting the disturbances to Prime Minister Pitt, Orde insisted that 'some regular and decisive amendment must be made in the Police, for it is impossible yet to foresee, that a new Mob may not in an instant renew the disturbances.[41] The Chief Secretary wished that a strong law against tumultuous meetings, as he explained to Pitt, would mean that 'we need not put such force into the plan which is to follow' for a strengthened police force.[42] In 1786 Orde concentrated on reforming the Dublin police, especially by way of centralization, and moving from the six wards to entire control from Dublin Castle. Based on three models of urban police he had before him,

---

Orde, who was once again afflicted with an eye inflammation that impaired his administrative effectiveness ...' Kelly, *Prelude to Union ...*, 179.

38 H.M.C. *The Manuscripts of the Duke of Beaufort*, 345; Cited in McElroy, 14–15.

39 H.M.C. *The Rutland Manuscripts*, III, 362. Cited in McElroy, 15.

40 Stanley H. Palmer, *Police and Protest in England and Ireland 1780–1850*, 93.

41 Orde to Pitt, 25, 28 August 1784, PRO 30/8/329/86/109-10. Quoted in Palmer, *Police and Protest ...*, 93.

42 Donnelly, 'Rightboy', 192.

he considered which one would be most suitable for Dublin; the London model, he deemed insufficient; the Edinburgh model, he considered but went for another option; the police system of Paris, he deemed most efficient, and decided that this model would be best for Dublin. On 20 March 1786, he introduced the government's 'Bill for the better Execution of the Law within the City of Dublin, and certain parts adjacent thereto'. The key to Orde's choice was that the Dublin police force would be centrally controlled within a single jurisdiction.[43] Orde also planned on reforming the rural police force, but it was only a blueprint for a later generation. In the 1830s Prime Minister Peel, conceived of a police force for Ireland, based on Orde's draft, to become known as 'Peelers'.[44]

Regardless of his lifelong bouts of illness, Orde achieved a remarkable level of output. During his three years in Dublin, he managed to include a revamping of Irish education on a national scale, and this was in addition to his regular portfolio as Chief Secretary. In the summer of 1786 he had one of his bouts of illness; went to Spa, and then to Bath, keeping all the time in touch with Irish affairs, but not certain whether he would be able to return to his duties in Ireland. He managed to do so at the end of November that year, but in the summer of 1787 he had a relapse 'suffering from extreme relaxation and nervous affliction'. The Duke of Rutland (Lord Lieutenant of Ireland) wrote to Pitt, the Prime Minister, informing him of Orde's ailments:

> Mr. Orde's health has been sacrificed to his zealous exertions … in the service of the public, where … his diligent and conscientious exertions have not been useless. His conduct has, in no instance, been distinguished by any inclination towards objects of emolument, nor has he shown any aspiration after rewards.[45]

Upon taking up his post as Chief Secretary in 1784 Thomas Orde was landed with an educational regime that was nothing more than a jumbled mixture of irregular and differing types of schools, all without any

43 Stanley H. Palmer, *Police and Protest in England and Ireland 1780–1850* (Cambridge: Cambridge University Press, 1988), 99.

44 See Palmer, 139.

45 Rutland to Pitt, *The History of Parliament: The House of Commons, 1754–1790*, vol. iii, 409. Also, 322–323 and 399.

particular supervisory body in charge. In a word the situation could be described as 'disordered' or even haphazard. Yes, there were many schools in the country, providing an abundance of learning at varying levels, from the downright basic and fundamental to the exalted and lofty, with an immense collection of the mediocre in between. As Orde alluded to the existing arbitrary and slapdash array of schools by claiming, 'nothing can be more fruitless or preposterous than the arrangements at present subsisting in several of the principal features of the scheme of education', he specified that 'the interference of government therefore is necessary, with the combined aid of the legislature'.[46]

The state had attempted education legislation in the past but, with little genuine fruitful results.[47] There were enthusiastic proselytizers who established schools, not always for the right reasons, and many of these existed in a state of chaotic turmoil. By the time Orde took up office in Ireland, these schools, though supported by government generosity, had floundered under the weight of indifference and neglect. Irish education, it would seem, was suffering from a malady and mired in the doldrums without a steward. The network of schools which had the greatest number attending were the pay schools (hedge schools), and they represented Catholic Ireland which had the greatest number of followers by far, were completely ignored by Orde. He did, however, offer the Catholics and Presbyterians[48] a certain level of lip-service suggesting they would be welcome to attend his Church of Ireland controlled new school system.

46 J. Giffard, *Mr. Orde's Plan of an Improved System of Education in Ireland,* 12 April 1787, House of Commons, College Green, Dublin.

47 In England, a non-interventionist state laissez-faire policy existed with regard to education provision. 'The less law, the more liberty' was the prevailing philosophy. See David Thomson, *England in the Nineteenth Century* (London: Penguin Books, 1970), 31. And, as Akenson puts it, 'England was a nation dependent on informal means of education for the civilisation of the bulk of its population.' See D. H. Akenson, *The Irish Education Experiment …*, 6.

48 Presbyterians also developed a network of hedge schools.

Orde was not a frequent speaker in parliamentary debates, but he was hard-working, able and persevering, he was valued by his bosses, but was not popular, and, like the typical civil servant, ill-suited to the parliamentary arena. Orde was in the habit of declining offers until the Duke of Rutland, when appointed Lord Lieutenant of Ireland, approached him through Shelburne:

> I should feel myself most particularly obliged to your Lordship if you would use your interposition with Mr. Orde to prevail on him to accept the office of secretary. It is an object of the last importance to the country in the present crisis, that a person of his character and ability should be employed in that situation.[49]

Orde was educated at Eton and at Cambridge, where he graduated with a BA in 1770 and an MA in 1773. Following his time at Cambridge, he was admitted to Lincoln's Inn, London, and was called to the Bar in 1775, the same year in which he became a Fellow of the Society of Antiquaries. In 1778 Thomas Orde married Jean Mary Browne-Powlett, daughter of Harry Powlett, sixth Duke of Bolton. Upon the death of Orde's father-in-law in 1794, his wife inherited the estate and Orde took the name Powlett in 1795. Little is known of Orde's formative years apart from his propensity for artistic sketching. While at Cambridge, he indulged in etching and this passion was to remain with him throughout his life, and especially satirical etchings.[50] At Cambridge, he also 'etched portraits of local persons'.[51]

49 Bolton Manuscripts, Rutland to Shelburne, 1 February 1784. See L. Namier and J. Brooke, eds, *The History of Parliament: House of Commons, 1754–1790.*

50 Cited in C. McElroy, *Thomas Orde 1746–1807: Educational Innovator* (Unpublished M.Ed., Thesis, submitted to University College Dublin, 1994), 10.

51 J. A. Venn, *Alumni Cantabrigienses,* pt. 2, vol. 4. Kahlenberg-Oyler (Cambridge: Cambridge University Press, 1951). Republished by CUP in 2012.

Figure 1: Orde and the Fruitseller

No doubt his legal training stood him in good stead later in life, especially when he was appointed Chief Secretary[52] for Ireland. On 18 February 1784, Orde went with Rutland to Ireland; and there he learnt on 27 March from George Rose that he would be returned for Harwich, a safe Treasury borough.[53]

52 Poynings' Law (1494) meant that the Irish Parliament lacked an independent power of legislation, and the Crown kept control of executive authority in the hands of the Lord Lieutenant and his appointees, such as the Chief Secretary, rather than in the hands of ministers responsible to the Irish Parliament.

53 See *The History of parliament ..., 1754–1790.*

Orde was 35 years old when he began service under Rutland, who was 30 years of age. Charles Manners, the Fourth Duke of Rutland, was a convivial young nobleman who had been elected at the age of 20 to the English House of Commons. Thomas Orde had nothing like Rutland's advantages of birth. However, he came from the propertied classes but untitled ranks of English society. He had none of the brilliance of Pitt as a political animal; in Sir Jonah Barrington's assessment, Orde was a hard-working, 'cautious, slow man, tolerably well-informed, but not at all talented'.[54]

Though the Irish parliament was granted a semblance of independence in 1782, and though it was distinctive from Westminster, it was still a subordinate parliament in a subordinate kingdom. The 1782 legislation left the connection between the two kingdoms dangerously vague and imprecise. Its 'independence' was not absolute, as policy arrangements were still being dealt with in London, to be executed by the Lord Lieutenant and his Chief Secretary, and whose responsibility lay with the British cabinet, and not the Irish parliament. In practice this meant that these two individuals were concerned with maintaining a sufficient body of government supporters in the Irish parliament to undertake the necessary steps with regard to policy implementation. The rebellion of 1798, and the national crisis it caused, meant that the British cabinet could see no better way of achieving stability other than dispensing with the Irish parliament.[55] There had been previous voices raised concerning a union during the second half of the eighteenth century, namely on one occasion when it was in relation the proposed Anglo-Irish trade agreement in which Orde was involved. Such voices were usually dismissed as being 'premature', as it was suggested that the Irish parliament would not vote itself out of existence.[56] Ironically, the Irish parliament was reluctant to grant concessions to Catholics, while the Westminster Cabinet was considering some form of emancipation for

54 Quoted in Stanley H. Palmer, *Police and Protest in England and Ireland, 1780–1850* (Cambridge: Cambridge University Press, 1990), 94.

55 J. L. McCracken, *The Irish Parliament in the Eighteenth Century* (Dundalk: Irish Historical Association, 1971), 22–4. See also, Patrick Geoghegan, *The Irish Act of Union: A Study in High Politics, 1798–1801* (Dublin: Gill and Macmillan, 1999).

56 Thomas Bartlett, *Ireland: A History* (Cambridge: Cambridge University Press, 2010), 227.

Catholics long before it transpired in 1829. Orde, in the 1780s, had no such plans as he was steadfastly in favour of an education system for Ireland which would be controlled and managed by the Church of Ireland and, hopefully, be of benefit to all classes and creeds.

As the eighteenth century came to a close, Ireland was still without a properly functioning education system; Orde's attempt at introducing one had failed; the hodge podge arrangement of hedge schools and Protestant society schools still continued, and without an indigenous parliament in Dublin, Ireland, in the nineteenth century had to rely more than ever on policies emerging from London.

The following chapters encapsulate the Irish educational landscape in Orde's time, along with the state of education in Ireland during the later decades of the eighteenth century. His inheritance and the evolution of his ideas on education are examined. Chapter Four emphasizes Orde's chief outlines for a plan of education for Ireland, followed by reactions to his plan. A short Postscript, dealing with Diocesan Schools, Royal Schools and Charter Schools, is also included.

The Hely-Hutchinson Plan for Irish Education

The Provost of the University of Dublin, with its one college, had represented the city of Cork in parliament; Hely-Hutchinson was also both Keeper of the Privy Seal and Secretary of State. He was an intimate friend of Edmund Burke, and at the end of 1786 he was appointed a Privy Councillor of Great Britain. From a political point of view, it is safe to say that he was a figure of considerable influence.[57] Hely-Hutchinson, who had befriended Orde prior to his first communication with him on the question of education, 'was a proponent of parliamentary reform and of relief of Catholic disabilities who also concerned himself with educational matters'.[58] James Kelly describes the Provost of TCD as a 'restless,

57 See C. McElroy, *Thomas Orde, 1746–1807: Educational Innovator …*, 44.

58 See D. H. Akenson, *The Irish Education Experiment*, 60.

ambitious, and not always trustworthy politician', but he 'interested himself in educational matters to such an extent that he was one of the most advanced and informed contemporary thinkers on the subject'.[59]

In October 1783 he had addressed the Irish House of Commons on the topic of education, saying that he had 'long seen the necessity of two or more great public schools, similar to Westminster and Eton, being established in this kingdom'.[60] He had also called for an investigation into the Charter School System, following John Howard's tour of these schools in 1783.[61] Howard[62] was adamant that the lower orders could be extricated from the situations in which they were living, and he was particularly keen on having the poor taught the principles of morality, and like many others including Orde and Hely-Hutchinson, to children of both sexes and all denominations.[63] The Provost glanced over a scheme he intended to propose, for establishing great schools in Ireland, and said at a convenient day he would bring it before the House.[64] Howard's criticism of the existing schools became a decisive influence on contemporary debate on educational matters.[65]

Hely-Hutchinson persisted, and in November 1783 he expressed his interest in the Irish House of Commons in having public schools for young

59 James Kelly, 'The Context and Course of Thomas Orde's Plan of Education of 1787', *The Irish Journal of Education* XX/1 (1986), 3–26, 6.

60 Quoted in Colm McElroy, *Thomas Orde, 1746–1807 ...*, 44.

61 D. L. Howard, *John Howard: Prison Reformer* (London: Johnson, 1958), 29.

62 Howard, like Jeremiah Fitzpatrick, was prominent prison reformer. Prison Reform had begun in Ireland in 1763 with the passing of the *Irish Acquitted Prisoners' Act.* Howard caused the first statute on prison reform in Britain to be passed in 1774, and this legislation was, in substance, aping its earlier Irish counterpart. See Oliver MacDonagh, *The Inspector General: Sir Jeremiah Fitzpatrick and Social Reform, 1783–1802* (London: Croom Helm, 1981).

63 *The Life of John Howard, Esquire: The Philanthropist* (Edinburgh, 1825; Anonymous). Reprinted by Palala Press, USA, 2015).

64 In the event, he never did, but Orde took up where Hely-Hutchinson failed to complete the work, and presented it as part of a wider package to the House in April 1787. See C. McElroy, *Thomas Orde ...*, 44.

65 See James Kelly, 'The Context and Course of Thomas Orde's Plan of Education of 1787', *The Journal of Education* 20/1 (1986), 3–26, 7.

gentlemen. He moved that a committee be appointed to enquire into the state of the existing public schools in Ireland. This was duly established, and on 17 December 1785, he sent his *Plan for a great school connected with the university* to Orde for his perusal.

Communications between the Provost of Trinity College and Thomas Orde had profound influence on the latter when it came to formulating his ideas on a reformed education system for Ireland. It could be claimed that the Provost acted as a catalyst on Orde, and, thus culminating in Orde's own extravagant and grandiose plan of 1787.

According to McElroy's research, Orde made notes in pencil on the blank side of the pages Hely-Hutchinson had sent him, and later he wrote out the whole document using ink. Orde also presented these notes to the Duke of Rutland, the Lord Lieutenant, and he was as impressed as Orde upon their reading of them. 'I am inclined to think the general system proposed is good',[66] he exclaimed.

A brief examination of Hely-Hutchinson's plan for a 'great school' linked with Trinity College is in order at this juncture. Orde's plan of 1787 went far ahead of the Provost's intimations from the years just preceding Orde's long speech in the Commons in College Green in 1787. However, the Provost's 'Outlines' did engender in Orde a certain stimulus for engaging with the establishment of 'great schools' or 'feeder schools' that would supply students to Ireland's one and only university. It was deemed essential to have such schools as the existing system was not producing scholars of merit because of the defective nature of the status quo. In order to remedy this situation, one great school was proposed by Hely-Hutchinson to cater for the most able of boys. Entrance to this school would be by competition and the students within would have the royal-sounding title of King's Scholars. The school would be all found, catering for all the needs of the students; education; dinner; supper; dormitory, and all without any expense.[67] The teachers should be imported from Eton, Westminster, Winchester or Harrow. As Latin was a pre-eminent subject

66 See page 45 in McElroy. H.M.C. 12th Report, Appendix 9, Letter from Thomas Orde to John Hely-Hutchinson, 26 December 1785.

67 Bolton Manuscripts, 15,884.

of study at the time, the masters would examine the potential student's standard of Latin. Each potential student to the great school was required to submit both Latin verse and prose for assessment.

The students who managed to find a place in Trinity College were to be known as King's Students. Hely-Hutchinson undertook a lot of work in fine-tuning his plans for a great school. It should be not less than forty miles from Dublin; it should be on the banks of a large river; the nearest town should be neat and well-regulated, where:

> There may be proper accommodation for masters, assistants, and dames' houses, and for French fencing and dancing masters, and where a temporary schoolhouse may be taken and the business of the school carried on.[68]

The Provost also costed the expense of such an enterprise, and surmised that the total annual outlay would not surpass £2,200.

Included in his plans was the purchase of land upon which would be built the houses for the accommodation of the above-mentioned staff members. While this era was before the age of school inspectors (the first being John Veevers, who did this job for the Kildare Place Society in 1818) the Provost, nonetheless, provided for school visitors in his plan. These visitors were to be given the task of school inspection and also settling any disputes. And, as for the curriculum in his planned school, Hely-Hutchinson had the following remarks to make:

> In the new school, the learned languages would be well taught. Young men would acquire the habits of composing, with ease and elegance. The habits of composition would make them read the principal authors with greater skill, care and attention; and reading in that manner would improve their composition; and both together would establish an accurate, critical, classical taste, in this great school.[69]

Such then was the narrow, classical curriculum of his great school, a curriculum, based on Latin composition which would prepare the students for life in the University of Dublin. And, when the King's Student, having secured a scholarship for a seven-year bursary in the university,

68 Bolton Manuscripts, 15,884. Cited in McElroy, 48.
69 Bolton Manuscripts, Ms. 15,884.

would henceforth be called a 'Select Student'. These 'Select Students' would become very accomplished in society, because they could avail of Trinity's opportunistic provision of studies in Spanish, German, Italian and French. This would enable them to enter any 'department of life' and society should, as a consequence of their high level of learning be in a position to command respect and in some instances they should be in position of political power. This scenario was, of course, reminiscent of Plato's concept of philosopher/king, where a political leader should be a learned individual if he or she is to make decisions that would be of benefit to the whole of society.

One aspect of Hely-Hutchinson's proposals on education reform was his pre-dating Thomas Wyse's emphasis on a legislative underpinning for all sectors of education provision. One of the greatest advantages of all following a reformed education system would be to:

> … raise the spirits and invigorate the exertions of the rising generation, to see that education is to become an object of public attention and solicitude, in Ireland, and that, by the cheering countenance of royal favour and protection, it is to receive legislative encouragement and support.[70]

Hely-Hutchinson had a feeder system in mind for Trinity College, something along the lines of the public schools in England. Nicholas Hans undertook a study of the link between the universities and the feeder schools in England.[71] In his research, he demonstrates very clearly the connection between the Public Schools in England and the universities. His figures prove indisputably that these schools supplied almost one-third of the élite in England of the eighteenth century and that of this amount the two schools Eton and Westminster had the lion's share. In Ireland, the connection between the Provost's plans and Orde's speech on education reform in the Irish House of Commons in 1787 is palpable.

70 Bolton Manuscripts, Ms. 15,884.

71 The elite public schools which acted as feeder schools for the universities were: Eton, Harrow, Rugby, Charterhouse, Shrewsbury, Winchester, Westminster, St. Paul's and Merchant Taylors. See Nicholas Hans, *New Trends in Education in the Eighteenth Century* (London: Routledge and Kegan Paul, 1951), 19. A new edition published by Routledge in 2013.

Within the same document Hely-Hutchinson made an additional proposal to Orde, advising him on the universal aspect of education in Ireland, but he honed in on the English (Primary) and Diocesan (Secondary) schools. He outlined a policy of state subvention for these schools as well as the Erasmus Smith and Charter Schools. He also harped back in time to pursue a rejuvenation policy for Tudor legislation with regard to Parish and Diocesan Schools, in so far as that:

> … every parish clergyman [should] keep … school pursuant to the statute of the 28. Henry 8, chap. 15 …. [This] may possibly be promoted by looking into the state of the Diocesan Free Schools, and enquiring whether the several acts of parliament on that subject have been properly executed ….[72]

Upon receipt of the Provost's schemes Orde took them earnestly, which is apparent in his notes. For example, his Observations with references to the sketch of a Plan for establishing Public Schools and introducing a better method of Education indicate very forcibly what he feels about the Provost's ideas.[73] Hely-Hutchinson had added to his earlier contribution to the discourse on education with another document dealing with the number of tutors and he suggested ways by which their number could be increased. The key aspect of the Provost's proposals was the extension of a Collegiate School or 'Great' School to Trinity College. The Provost, of course, could have been accused of prejudice in favour of the extension to his own institution rather than any philanthropic notions about the sorry state of Irish education. Nonetheless, it is very clear that the two, the Provost of the University of Dublin and the Chief Secretary for Ireland, had a mutual respect for one another's ideas on the future educational developments in Ireland. When we examine Orde's speech of 1787, it is evident that it is peppered with references to Hely-Hutchinson's understanding of the role the Public Schools (or the 'great school' in Ireland) can play in the supply of elite students to the universities.

72 Bolton Manuscripts, Ms. 15884.

73 Bolton Manuscripts, Ms. 15885.

CHAPTER 2

The Irish Educational Landscape in Orde's Time: Contextual Analysis

Introduction

The Ireland of the eighteenth century witnessed a rising population; there was considerable political unease, with underground subversive organizations creating a great deal of discomfort for the government; Grattan's Parliament was ostensibly an independent parliament running an independent state but, in reality, it offered only a pastiche of independence; ordinary people (mainly Catholic) were merely surviving from the crumbs of the table of education (the official education patchwork of schools was entirely of the Established Church, while the Catholic population had their own Pay Schools or Hedge Schools).[1] Though there was a form of 'independence', the actual administration remained in the hands of the Lord Lieutenant who was appointed by the English government. This chapter deals with the two educational traditions in Ireland; it also address the existence of education plans other than Orde's; it treats of Orde and education; the Penal laws and their significance is addressed; the end of the chapter has a section on concluding remarks.

In the eighteenth-century Ireland possessed at least two educational traditions, one was private and the other state-initiated. It is easy to deal with the state sector first: in 1537 Henry VIII had a law passed that provided

1 Antonia McManus, *The Irish Hedge School and Its Books, 1695–1831* (Dublin: Four Courts Books, 2002).

for parish schools throughout the country. On paper, this piece of Tudor legislation looked very promising, but the King's writ did not count for much beyond the Pale,[2] resulting in many shortcomings within the parish school network.

Under this legislation schools were to be established in each parish and run by the local Anglican clergy. The aim was to consolidate English political advances by encouraging the youth of Ireland to adopt English ways and customs, including, above all, the language. Beyond the counties of Dublin, Meath and Louth, 'the English tongue is turned into the Irish tongue, that it is expedient that every lord and gentleman within these counties be constrained to put their children to cities and towns where they may learn English speech.'[3] This situation was addressed by legislation in the Irish parliament. This legislation provided for the preservation of English cultural, religious and political interests in the country. Section three of the Act stated:

> That every person or persons, the King's true subjects, inhabiting this land of Ireland … shall use and speake [sic] commonly the English tongue and language, and that every such person … having childe or children, shall endeavour themselves to cause and procure his said childe and children to use and speake the English tongue and language, and … shall bring up and keep his said childe and children in such places, where they shall or may have occasion to learn the English tongue, language, order and condition.[4]

Another section, the ninth, enacted that all churchmen with the authority to confer orders should first obtain a sworn understanding from the candidates for orders that they would make every effort to learn English

2 The Pale was effectively an English area of administration in Ireland. It consisted of a narrow strip of land, thirty miles wide, encompassing modern day County Dublin and parts of Kildare, Meath and Louth. The remainder of the country was 'governed' by Anglo-Irish nobility or native Irish families, the Fitzgeralds and the O'Connors of Munster being two examples.

3 James Godkin, *Education in Ireland: Its history, Institutions, Systems, and Progress, from the Earliest Times to the Present* (London: Saunders, Otley and Co., 1862), 16.

4 T. Corcoran, *State Policy in Irish Education, A.D. 1536 to 1816* (Dublin: Fallon Brothers, 1916), 43.

themselves and that they would conduct all praying and preaching in English:

> … and also shall keepe, or cause to be kept, within the place, territory, or parish, where he shall have … benefice or promotion, a schole for to learn English, if any children of his parish come to him to learn the same, taking for the keeping of the same schole, such convenient stipend or salarie, as in the said land is accustomably used to be taken.[5]

In essence, this legislation was an effort to shore up the loyalty of the Anglo-Irish, and it was not aimed specifically at the native Irish.[6] A network of parish schools was to be created. This legislation was the first to provide an infrastructure for both anglicization and proselytization. The lack of success with the parish schools led the Crown to revisit the problem of education in Ireland, this time with a different type of school. Queen Elizabeth's 1570 legislation for grammar-school-type education made way for the establishment of diocesan schools. These schools for the middle classes were equally useless as the Parish Schools, and differed little from them, except that it was made definite in the Act 12 Elizabeth c.1 'that the schoolmaster shall be an Englishman or of the English birth in this realm'.[7] Dr Kyle, Secretary to the Commissioners of Education, and in a retrospective fame of mind, stated before the Royal Commission (Powis) on Primary Education, on 24 October 1868, that 'the whole system of Diocesan Schools is perfectly and completely rotten'.[8]

Closer to Orde's time, the 1791 Commissioners' Report found that the system of diocesan schools was inadequate:

> From this institution, the public receives very inadequate benefit; in many dioceses, there neither diocesan schools nor schoolhouses; in many the houses are ruinous and the mastership [sic] were sinecures.[9]

5 T. Corcoran, *State Policy in Irish Education …*, 43.
6 D. H. Akenson, *The Irish Education Experiment,* 22.
7 J. J. Auchmuty, *Irish Education,* 64.
8 Michael O' Riordan, *Catholicity and Progress* (London: K. Paul, Trench, Trubner and Co., 1906), 127–128.
9 *Report of the Commissioners 1791,* Appendix, 1, p. 4.

In all these Acts and in subsequent reinforcement of them, we witness the direct effort of governments to provide educational facilities for sections of the community. We see the complete failure of this policy and the general realization of the hopelessness of the attempt. Grants were made, not to these schools but to those which were founded by the various charitable organizations. Unfortunately, here the objectives were different, and the action of the government in this respect led to difficulties which later were to prove vital factors in the smooth working of the National System.

Legacy

When we get to Orde's time, we find that only 352 parish schools are in existence out of a total of 1,669 parishes that came under surveyance.[10] The Anglican clergy had little or no say in the running of these schools, under the 1537 Act, they were held responsible for so doing. There was a great deal of corruption associated with the management of these schools. In no instance in the survey carried out by the commissioners in 1788 was the incumbent Anglican clergyman in charge of a school. Instead a deputy was paid for that purpose.[11] Many felt that these schools were little more than proselytizing agencies:

> As the system emerged it became increasingly clear that the eighteenth-century reality did not match the sixteenth-century theory. This was because the conditions referred to in the 1537 act had all but vanished along with the distinction between the Pale and the mere Irish. Whereas the Tudor statute focused upon the teaching of the English language and customs, the renewing acts emphasized the advancement of the Protestant religion. As the schools became identified as proselytizing agencies, Catholics grew reluctant to enrol their children.[12]

10 *Report of the Commissioners of Irish Education Inquiry, 1791, for the year 1788.*

11 See T. Corcoran, *State Policy in Irish Education* (Dublin: Fallon Brothers, 1916), 167–172.

12 D. H. Akenson, *The Irish Education Experiment,* 24.

In short, these schools had failed, and it was Orde who took it upon himself and used his high office as Chief Secretary to re-energize these schools, both parish and diocesan, in the hope that the aims of the originators would be fulfilled centuries later. This was a Protestant scheme for a Protestant people. Catholics or Dissenters had no part to play unless they turned and 'took the shilling'.[13]

Though there were two separate aspects to this Tudor legislation, the outcome was not satisfactory from the state's point of view. Only a handful of schools under Tudor legislation ever came into being. This was the first occasion when a system of secondary education was formalized under an Elizabethan act for the establishment of a free grammar school in the principal town in each diocese. However, these schools catered for only a handful of pupils. When we reach Orde's time, his policy was to ensure the existence of twenty-two of these diocesan schools throughout the country.

There was considerable opposition to the 1570 Elizabethan act, and this often stemmed from those who had to foot the bill. A few short years following the act, we find Sir John Perrott, Lord Deputy, in 1584 indicating that the Schools Act of 1570 was inoperative when he said, 'we find that free schools, which are to be maintained and kept for the education and bringing up of youth in good literature, are now, for the most part, not kept or maintained.'[14] And to rub salt into the wounds, it was found that in the whole country only twenty Diocesan schoolmasters were found and six of these, though in receipt of their salary, did not teach at all.[15] Michael Quane gives a clear exposition of the intolerable conditions under which some of these schools operated. For example, the Diocesan School of Clogher was merely 'a schoolroom, which had neither floor nor ceiling'.[16]

By Orde's time in Ireland, only fourteen of the Diocesan schools were in operation, with a grand total of 324 students in attendance. The total number of boarders in these schools was forty-six. Akenson attests to the

13 See Akenson, *The Irish Education Experiment*, 22.

14 Michael Quane, 'The Diocesan Schools – 1570–1870', *Journal of the Cork Historical and Archaeological Society* (Jan.–June 1961), 31.

15 Corcoran, *State Policy in Irish Education*, 157. See also C. McElroy, *Thomas Orde, 1746–1807*, 27–29.

16 Michael Quane, 'The Diocesan Schools – 1570–1870', 38.

prevalence of children of the middle classes attending these schools.[17] These schools were often of little use to the poor, and with so few students were of little use to society. Reform was of immediate concern, and Orde, once he began his education quest in Ireland, was particularly anxious about reinvigorating these schools.

A second aspect of endowed schools came under the wing of private enterprise, namely the Erasmus Smith Schools.[18] The Charter Schools were an eighteenth-century phenomenon whose expressed object was to take the children of the poor and bring them up as Protestants, came into being in the 1830s. These schools were relatively successful.

Erasmus Smith was a Cromwellian soldier who bequeathed funds to be used in his name for the upkeep of schools in Ireland. It was stipulated that these schools should bear his name. These schools never matched expectations, and by the time we reach the second half of the eighteenth-century state policy regarding anglicization and proselytization was in dismal circumstances. And, as we have seen elsewhere, funds for the Erasmus Smith Schools was being diverted, as Corcoran points out; '... in the eighteenth century a considerable part of the rental of the Erasmus Smith Estates was diverted to the University from its original purpose ...'[19]

As far as popular education was concerned, these schools were too few in number to contribute in any significant manner towards providing a country-wide education system. They fell short on success on many perceived fronts. The country, in the late eighteenth century, with a population of four millions required a vastly greater number of schools to serve

17 D. H. Akenson, *The Irish Education Experiment,* 27.

18 Erasmus Smith (1611–1691) was granted extensive property under the Settlement of Ireland Act of 1652 as repayment for his support for the suppression of the 1641 Rebellion, and he proposed in 1655 that some the monies from the lands be used to endow 'five school-houses for the teaching of grammar and the original tongue'. A trust established in 1657 was styled 'The Governors of the Schools Founded by Erasmus Smith'. In 1666 the number of proposed schools was reduced to three – Drogheda, Galway and Tipperary – but unexpectedly high dividends a century later meant that, in addition to supporting a Charter School in Sligo, in 1773 the governors resolved to build a school 'in or near the Town of Ennis'. See D. Murphy, 'Erasmus Smith House', *History Ireland* 31/3 (May–June 2023), 33.

19 T. Corcoran, *State Policy* ... 14.

its needs. It is estimated that combined these schools catered for less than 14,000 pupils. Of these, about 13,000 were primary school pupils. Though there was a great draw on government resources to fund these schools, the return often seemed paltry. One of the chief concerns was a litany of abuses associated with the parish schools of Henry VIII and the Diocesan Schools of his daughter Elizabeth I. It was found that much of the monies granted to the local Anglican clergy to run these schools was being diverted to other areas within the Established Church. It appears that the words corruption, diversion, detour and possibly swingling are some of key concepts associated with the provision of education in Ireland under Tudor legislation, and under some private enterprise.[20] According to Akenson, there may have been no parish schools at all in the country the reign of Henry the Eight.[21] In his estimation, parish schools only began appearing in the early decades of the eighteenth century.

As the system emerged, it became increasingly clear that the eighteenth-century reality did not match the sixteenth-century theory. The conditions had altered in the intervening years, and the distinction between the Pale and the 'mere' Irish had vanished. The Tudor statute focused on the teaching of the English language and customs, while the renewing acts emphasized the promotion of the Protestant religion. As the schools became identified as proselytizing agencies, the Catholic population became reluctant to enrol their children.

20 For example, the Erasmus Smith Fund paid every year for three fellows, thirty-five exhibitions for poor scholars, a professor of mathematics and two assistants, a professor of oriental languages and two assistants, a professor of oratory and one assistant, a professor of history and one assistant and a professor of natural and experimental philosophy. See McElroy, *Thomas Orde, 1746–1807 …*, 33, footnote.

21 Akenson, 23.

Catholic Schools

Alongside this Protestant educational network was the Catholic private free enterprise matrix of pay schools, popularly known as hedge schools. These schools catered for the vast majority of the school-going population of Ireland, but they never received any recognition from the state. On occasions, the Catholic hierarchy had many misgivings about these schools.

Though some of the schools were non-exclusive, Catholics and Presbyterians were unable, because of their religious beliefs and practices, to benefit from them. To this end both dissenting groups, Presbyterians as well as Catholics, carried on their own type of private education. For about one hundred and fifty years, from the end of the seventeenth century to the middle of the nineteenth, the main source of education for the rural poor was the hedge school. In a manner, this patchwork of schools emerged from the peasantry as a response to attempts at suppression of their rights. It became, in many ways, an act of defiance and it meant that they paid for their children's education. The fact that payment was involved also meant that the poorest of the poor never took part in hedge school education.[22]

Because of penal legislation from the late seventeenth century onwards Catholics and Presbyterians and any dissenting religious groups were not allowed to have an education which did not subscribe to the tenets of Anglicanism. However, as the eighteenth progressed, these laws were relaxed and by century's end, Catholics could openly attend Catholic schools.

By the time Thomas Orde arrived on Irish shores in 1784 there was a chequered collection of educational institutions, many of which had come into existence on a distinctly ad hoc basis.

The task ahead for Orde must have seemed daunting, nay impossible, but if anything he proved to be persistent and persuasive, after his own fashion.

22 See Tony Lyons, 'Hedge Schools of Kerry', *Journal of the Kerry Archaeological and Historical Society* 2/4 (2004), 133–152.

There were numbers of individuals who put forward various types of plans for Irish education during the closing decades of the eighteenth century. One thing they had in common was a recognition of the failure of previous attempts to introduce a nationwide network of schools at various levels. It was Jeremy Bentham's wish to improve the lot of the Irish people through an education system. Bentham had two plans in mind, one for Ireland and another for Irish labourers in New York. Though Bentham's plans were very laudable, his utilitarianism did not aid in his abiding with the plans for very long.[23] Another educationist, with many interests, was Richard Lovell Edgeworth,[24] who had a grand plan for education in Ireland. But, not unlike Bentham, he too did not stay with his ideas for very long or until they came to fruition.[25] The closing decades of the eighteenth century proved to be a remarkable era of political, economic and social change. The period of the Industrial Revolution and the Enlightenment[26] fostered a ferment of innovative thinking about many issues in society. It was an age of optimism, whereby new ideas found space for cultivation and advancement. The potential of new ideas and inventions became part of this newfound spirit. Richard Lovell Edgeworth shared in this *weltanschauung* and his curious, inventive, experimental cast of mind, as well as his pro-active,

23 See Brian W. Taylor, 'Jeremy Bentham and the Education of the Irish People', *The Irish Journal of Education* 14/1 (1980), 19–32.

24 Edgeworth was a formidable Enlightenment figure who proposed an education plan at the end of the end of the eighteenth century. He and his daughter, Maria, opened a school at Edgeworthstown, County Longford, and it flourished until his death in 1817. Maria kept the school open until 1834, but with dwindling numbers and considerable financial constraints.

25 Tony Lyons, *The Education Work of Richard Lovell Edgeworth, Irish Educator and Inventor, 1744–1817* (New York: Mellen Press, 2003).

26 It refers to an intellectual movement pre-dominant in the eighteenth century. The thinkers of the Enlightenment were referred to as 'philosophes' in France, and they professed a secular view of looking at the world. Reason and rationality were the twin bedfellows upon which human understanding gained supremacy over faith. These thinkers considered themselves as continuing the work of Locke, Bacon, Galileo, Newton Leibnitz, Descartes, and others who had developed fruitful methods of rational and empirical inquiry. Their writings placed science in a pivotal position in knowledge, and this should be extended to every field of human endeavour, including education.

practical approach to problems made him a representative exemplar of this movement. He had Renaissance qualities, with interests of a wide-ranging nature. These included mechanics, steam engines, coach building, road design and building, aerostatics, telegraph, land reclamation, legal reform, engineering and education. His acquaintances included Erasmus Darwin, Joseph Priestley, Jeremy Bentham, Josiah Wedgewood, William Godwin, Thomas Day, David Hartley, Joseph Lancaster and Jean-Jacques Rousseau. His reading included the works of John Locke, and the French *philosophes* of rational Enlightenment thinking. Edgeworth was also a prominent member of the Lunar Society of Birmingham, 'the friends who made the future'. Indeed, this company had many a philosophical feast!

Rationality

To put his ideas into practice, Edgeworth established a multi-denominational school at Edgeworthstown, County Longford, a school which welcomed children of different creeds. His treatise, *Practical Education* (1798), was well received throughout Europe and North America, being republished several times. He was also concerned with education in the public sphere; he sat on a number of boards of inquiry into the state of education in Ireland, and his attempted Education Bill of 1799 later formed the backbone of the National System of Education in Ireland (1831).

Believing in education as the great engine of progress, Edgeworth brought his education bill to Parliament on 28 March 1799, but it was ill-timed as the negotiations on the upcoming Act of Union took precedence over an education bill in parliamentary procedures. However, though the bill was not passed into law, some details are nevertheless worthy of inclusion here.

Following the arrival of Edgeworth in the Irish House of Commons, it was requested by the House that the 1791 Report be presented and that a committee be established to look into the state of Irish education with regard to the poorer classes.[27] Edgeworth took the bull by the horns

27 Burton, 25. Edward Burton suggests that the 1791 Report, though not published at

and presented his education bill to the House two weeks following the committee's establishment.

He addressed the House on 22 February 1799. He reported from the Committee that had been set up to examine the position of education regarding the lower orders in Ireland. In his speech there were six resolutions:

> First, the education of the poorer classes was declared to be highly defective, and legal intervention was called for.
>
> Second, one or more schools in each parish in the country should be introduced.
>
> Third, the teachers in these schools should be qualified and receive certificates in morals and ability, and obtain an annual licence.
>
> Fourth, payment of such teachers should consist of two types: a fixed salary, and an additional payment based on their exertions and their success. (This latter one was an example of 'payment by results')
>
> Fifth, that the books used in the schools be created locally and be chosen by persons appointed for that task.
>
> Sixth, these schools to be inspected at least once a year.[28]

The above resolutions were to be debated upon on the following Monday. Following this discussion it was agreed by the House that Edgeworth and three others should prepare a bill on the topic of education for the poorer classes in Ireland. Edgeworth's bill got one reading, but promised second never materialized. Akenson believes that it was the politics of the coming union with Great Britain that scuppered the education bill in 1799. Akenson also states that the exact contents of the bill is a mystery, as no copy remains.[29] However, Edward Burton maintains that the Edgeworth Papers contain some documents with the title 'A Bill for the Improvement of the Education of the lower Orders of people in this Kingdom',[30] dated 1799.

---

the time, but a draft form may have been made available to interested parties.

28 See D. H. Akenson, *The Irish Education Experiment ...*, 74–76.

29 Akenson, 75.

30 Edward Burton, 'Richard Lovell Edgeworth's Education Bill of 1799: A Missing Chapter in the History of Irish education', *Irish Journal of Education* XIII/1 (1979), 24–33.

Was there an official reason for dropping the Edgeworth Bill? The Chancellor of the Exchequer's response was reported in the *Dublin Evening Post:* the country was in a distracted state; public money was in short supply; it was better to wait until there was a state of greater 'tranquility', when the government should have more leisure and more power to complete a scheme of National Education.[31]

Edgeworth did not throw in the towel, as he led the 1806–1812 Commission on education, upon his appointment by the Lord Lieutenant. This commission produced fourteen reports, the fourteenth being the most productive of ideas and plans for education in Ireland during the new century. This was the second attempt at introducing a systematic scheme of education for Ireland, Thomas Orde's being the first. It is gratifying to note that Thomas Orde was not alone in promulgating a plan for Irish education during the last decades of the eighteenth century.

These new schools, Provincial Schools, were to be modelled on the English grammar schools, such as Christ's Hospital, London; he also had planned for an inspectorial system for the schools; he also had a second university in mind. When Orde put his plans before the Irish House of Commons, there was universal agreement for his proposals. However, his tenure of office in Ireland was cut short, when he was replaced as Chief Secretary. The Duke of Rutland (Charles Manners) also died before Orde left office, and with that death Orde had lost his great mentor for the post of Chief Secretary. Thus, his good work on education in Ireland was left in 'no man's land'. One aspect of his plans for education must be remembered is the fact that his plans did not provide for the majority population, which was Catholic. Though he often spoke about a universal system of education in Ireland, the exclusion of possibility eighty per cent of the population, by default or otherwise, must be taken on board when assessing the contribution Thomas Orde made to Irish education.

31 *Dublin Evening Post,* 2 April 1799. Cited in Burton, 'Richard Lovell Edgeworth's Education Bill of 1799' …., 30.

Nearing Orde's Plan

During Thomas Orde's tenure in Ireland as Chief Secretary, his first thoughts on education reform revolved about setting up a 'great school' or Collegiate School attached to the University of Dublin (Trinity College). Such a school was the brainchild of the Provost of Trinity, John Hely-Hutchinson, and both he and Orde were like-minded when it came to education reform or regeneration. This school would attract elite students from other post-primary schools in the country, and then it would act as a feeder school for Trinity College. Later, Orde came up with a much more sophisticated and comprehensive plan for Irish education, on a national scale. Crucially, he had hoped that a bill could be passed in the Irish Parliament to underpin his new scheme. This plan included the revitalization of existing schools and the launch of entirely new types on the Irish market.

Interestingly, the Provost of Trinity College, Dublin, John Hely-Hutchinson, proposed a plan of reform for Irish education in 1783 (as we have seen), and in his plan was the provision for 'great public schools' similar to Westminster and Eton. Having presented his proposals in the Irish House of Commons, he sent a detailed outline of his plans to the Chief Secretary for Ireland in the 1780s. In this communiqué he wrote:

> The want of good schools in this kingdom has long been the subject of general complaint. There never was greater cause for it than at present. The learned languages are very ill taught; and young men are not trained to composition in any language. The defects in school education essentially affect the knowledge, taste, and manner of the people.[32]

Hely-Hutchinson proposed two great schools for Ireland under the authority of legislation, and these schools were to be supported at public expense. He had other proposals for education in Ireland as well as the ones

32 Quoted in D. H. Akenson, *The Irish Education Experiment: The National System of Education in the Nineteenth Century* (London: Routledge and Kegan Paul, 1970), 60.

mentioned here. Thomas Orde was in a prime position to receive such detail from the Provost, as Orde was a member of the Irish Parliament for Rathcormack from 1784 to 1790, and he was also a member of the English Parliament from 1780 to 1796. It is very likely that Orde was influenced by Hely-Hutchinson in the realm of educational reform.[33]

On 17 December 1785 Hely-Hutchinson sent a long document to Orde entitled, 'Outline of a Plan for a Great School Connected with the University, and Some Thoughts on School Education in Ireland':

> As there is a significant and definite relationship between the proposals sent to Orde by Hely-Hutchinson and Orde's first tentative steps in College Green to introduce a bill concerning the question of education, it may be assumed that Hely-Hutchinson had a great deal more influence on the new Chief Secretary than anyone else.[34]

Perhaps, McElroy is correct but Akenson puts the relationship in a different light stating that 'Hely-Hutchinson's plan intrigued him'[35] (Orde). One thing is certain: Orde was fully aware of the contents of the Provost's plans for Irish education as expressed in 1785.

Orde and Education

Though, Orde's first interests in Ireland were concerned with the commercial union of both England and Ireland, Hely-Hutchinson's plan for Irish education aroused his curiosity. When Orde presented his plan for Irish education in the House of Commons, it was the Provost of Trinity College who seconded the motion.[36] It is, therefore, likely that Orde drew upon Hely-Hutchinson's earlier plan for Irish education.

33 Colm McElroy, *Thomas Orde, 1746–1807: Educational Innovator ...*, 43.

34 Colm McElroy, *Thomas Orde ...*, 43.

35 Akenson, 61.

36 See Akenson, *The Irish Education Experiment ...*, 60–62. Also, Áine Hyland and Kenneth Milne, eds, *Irish Educational Documents*, vol. 1 (Dublin: Church of Ireland College of Education, 1987), 55–58.

Thomas Orde-Powlett, 1st Baron Bolton (30 August 1740–30 July 1807) was an English politician. He also had a strong interest in artistic work, delving into etchings and cartoons. His father was John Orde of Northumberland.

Orde's appointment as Chief Secretary for Ireland in 1784 provided an opportunity for him to express his sense of commitment to raising the living standards of ordinary people. He was an active politician, and though he used his high office to explore the needs of a country vis à vis education requirements, his interests encompassed a broader scheme of things for Ireland as his concern for education was only one part of his extensive repertoire.

The interest of the Irish Parliament in education for all and a national system of education began with Orde, Chief Secretary for Ireland, and a member of both the Irish and English Parliaments. His proposals to the Irish Parliament in 1787 astounded many of the members, but it was approved by Parliament, though opposed by Catholics and Dissenters.[37] Debate continued and commissioners were appointed to investigate the educational situation in Ireland both before and after the Union.

William Pitt, 'the younger', 1783–1801, British Prime Minister was willing to enter into negotiations with Ireland in trade arrangements and to this end, Orde produced in 1785, what were to become known as 'Orde's Proposals' a plan to help trade arrangements between the two islands, and thus, improving the Irish economy. In practice, this meant a commercial union between Ireland and Britain. He presented his proposals to the Irish Parliament. There were eleven proposals: they advised that all foreign goods, including those from British Colonies, should pass freely between England and Ireland. All the products or manufactures of either country could be sent to the other, either without duty or at equal duties for both. When the English import was higher it should be lowered to the level of the Irish one. The proposals found favour in the Irish Parliament, but it was an entirely different story at Westminster. In order for Pitt to get the

37 Colm McElroy, 'Thomas Orde and Educational Innovation, 1786–1787', *Irish Educational Studies* 15/Spring (1996), 152–163; J. Kelly, 'The Context and Course of Thomas Orde's Plan of Education in 1787', *The Irish Journal of Education,* 20 (1986), 3–26.

proposals passed, he had to undertake modifications. Irish manufactures were to receive grants to aid in production of their goods, and markets in the Far East were made available to their exports. The fishing industry benefited, as did the manufactures of boots, shoes, blankets, soap and candles. Waterford Glass products became famous at home and abroad. The linen trade got a revived impetus, and found a ready market in the United States.[38] These commercial measures were geared towards placing 'Anglo-Irish economic relations on a firm, liberal, and permanent basis'.[39] In many ways the negotiations surrounding the commercial arrangements between the two countries paved the way for Orde playing the part of statesman; and so it was when he entered the Commons on College Green on Thursday, 12 April 1787, he found a very pliable and willing audience before him and his elaborate three-hour speech.

Pitt had been in favour of parliamentary reform for Ireland, but he was persuaded from Dublin Castle by Rutland[40] and Orde to leave the Irish system alone, and he duly subscribed to their views and turned his attention to the politics of the economy.

The moment he took up the post of Chief Secretary, Ireland was now Orde's dominant concern, and even when he attended Westminster during visits paid to London to discuss Irish affairs with ministers he made sure that the meetings were useful and meaningful. Thus he wrote to Rutland, 3 June 1784:

38 See M. Hayden and G. A. Moonan, *A Short History of the Irish People* Pt. 2 (Dublin: The Educational Company of Ireland, n.d.), 412–414.

39 Correspondence between the right hon. William Pitt and Charles, Duke of Rutland, lord lieutenant of Ireland, 1781–1787 (Edinburgh and London, 1890), 50. Quoted in R. B. McDowell, 'Parliamentary Independence, 1782–1789', in T. W. Moody and W. E. Vaughan, eds, *A New History of Ireland,* vol. 4. *Eighteenth-Century Ireland, 1691–1800* (Oxford University Press, 1986), 277.

40 Charles Manners succeeded as Fourth Duke of Rutland, and became Lord Lieutenant of Ireland in 1784. He advocated a union between the two countries. He was very popular among the Big Houses in Ireland, and was renowned for his hospitality at Dublin Castle.

> I have avoided taking my seat to-day as Sawbridge threatened a question upon reform of parliament, and I was afraid of misconstruction upon my conduct, in whatever way I might direct it, if it found its way into a Dublin newspaper.[41]

In Ireland the Chief Secretary became the 'first instrument of Administration', at a time when a re-modelling of Anglo-Irish relations was in the air. The kernel of this imperative was to grant Ireland commercial equality with Great Britain in return for an Irish contribution to Imperial financial outlay.

The Irish administration was troubled by the suggestion that Ireland should make an automatic contribution towards imperial defence. It would, Rutland was certain, 'kindle a flame ... against the English government and, I might also say, English connection'. 'Your idea of obtaining a revenue from Ireland in return for the concession of a full equality of commerce, was, he told Pitt, 'impracticable, inconsistent with the principles of true policy, and would, I fear, completely defeat the main object of your munificence, that of quieting faction and of constituting the foundations of a permanent good understanding between the two kingdoms'.[42] But, Pitt could not be dissuaded as he felt Ireland was getting so much – a guarantee of the colonial market; a firm place in the British market; and he was expecting a quid pro quo from the Irish administration. The debate went on.

Orde's political career had begun in earnest in 1780 when he was elected M.P. for Aylesbury, a position he held for four years before being returned for Harwich in 1784 and again in 1790. Promotion came fast. In 1782 he was appointed Under-Home Secretary and later that year was appointed Secretary to the Treasury.[43]

James Kelly claims that Orde lacked self-confidence as a public speaker, but was more adept at getting business done at committee level.[44] The Duke of Rutland, Lord Lieutenant of Ireland sponsored Orde to become

41 Quoted in L. Namier and J. Brooke, eds, *The History of Parliament ..., 1754–1790*.

42 See T. W. Moody and W. E. Vaughan, eds, *A New History of Ireland,* vol. IV (Oxford: Oxford University Press), 279.

43 See McElroy, 10.

44 J. Kelly, *Dictionary of Irish Biography* (2009).

Chief Secretary for Ireland from 1784 to 1787. Kelly paints a further psychological pen-picture of Orde when he writes:

> Orde had few equals in terms of sheer application, but he was an uninspiring and, at times, excessively cautious administrator who lacked confidence, sureness of judgement and social grace. More seriously, he wilted under pressure, and was inclined to self-pity at moments of crisis. Where hard work and application were sufficient, Orde ensured that business was conducted smoothly, but where political skill and imagination were necessary he was often found wanting.[45]

Orde was aware of the need for reform[46] of Irish education, as he was aware that Grattan's Parliament[47] had offered some relief to Catholics from the penal laws, but further relief was being arduously sought. Before Orde's plan for restructuring Irish education was put before the House in 1787, he had intimated some details to the members on occasions prior to that date. In his investigations he found instances where something was amiss at all levels of education and its provision. On a number of occasions Orde spoke of providing an education that would be universal and it would serve all communities. On the other hand, he declared that parish schoolmasters 'are to be protestants and so they ought to be, but this is also another impediment in some cases at present, where there is not an adequate inducement for a man to risk his safety'. He did recognize, though, that Catholics will not send their children to Protestant schools. Unfortunately, for Orde and his complex and urbane plans for

45 J. Kelly, *Prelude to Union: Anglo-Irish Politics in the 1780s* (Cork: Cork University Press, 1992), 78.

46 This was an age when there were political clubs, societies, pamphleteering and individuals in both England and Ireland who were clamouring for, not only education reform, but parliamentary reform as well. This was especially true of the 1770s and 1780s.

47 The Irish Parliament had two limitations on its powers: the English parliament claimed the right to legislate for Ireland; a restriction was imposed by one of its own statutes, Poynings' Law, 1495, where this law prevented the Irish Parliament from meeting until the Lord Lieutenant or the lord justices and the privy council had transmitted some bills to the king and the British privy council as a reason for summoning.

Irish education, he did not examine the situation from the Catholic point of view.

Penal Legislation

The Penal Laws were the dominant feature for the majority of the people during the eighteenth century, though historians differ on interpretations of the Code. Questions that may well be asked might include; were the laws implemented fully, and who did they effect most of all?; did Presbyterians feel the brunt of the laws as much as Catholics? Can any consensus be reached by those writing about the laws? What was the reason behind the laws? Ireland, with a Protestant Ascendancy Parliament sitting in College Green in Dublin passed these laws. Penal legislation did not affect the Anglican Church (Established Church or Church of Ireland), but, rather those who felt the brunt of the laws, at least in theory, were any religious group that did not subscribe to the official line of the Established Church. Such dissenters, then, were deemed to be outcasts or pariahs or undesirables, and who were not worthy of benefiting from the state's largesse. This included legislative protection, vis à vis individual rights; the laws tampered with Irish people and their level of citizenship, which in turn led to a denial of access to, for example, education. A whole swathe of people found themselves 'beyond the Pale' as it were, and this was in their own country. Were the laws anti-Popery in deed as much as in spirit? The laws were not always enforced, however, except, perhaps, in the 1740s when a Jacobite threat to stability was in the offing. With the defeat of the Jacobites in 1745 came something of a new Protestant dawn, a dawn which brought the laws right up to the final decades of the century.

The laws against education were contained in a Williamite Statute of 1695 entitled 'An Act to restrain foreign education'. By this Act of Parliament (Irish), Catholics were forbidden to send their children abroad for education. It was ruled that every person so doing, sending or sent:

> ... shall on conviction be disabled to sue in law or equity or to be a guardian, executor or administrator, or take a legacy or deed of gift, or bear any office, and shall forfeit goods and chattels for ever and land for life.[48]

And, it was further enacted that:

> ... no person whatsoever of the papist religion shall publicly teach school, or instruct youth in learning ...[49]

In 1709 these laws were extended to forbid Catholics to teach school in a private house or to become ushers or assistants in Protestant schools.

The aim of the penal laws was not to destroy Catholicism but to ensure that its adherents were kept in positions of social, economic and political inferiority, a position they retained throughout most of the eighteenth century. In short, this was tantamount to ethnic cleansing. If not ethnic cleansing, then it was deprivation on a massive scale. The position of the dominant minority could not be threatened. This, in some ways reflected the weakness and vulnerability of the minority Protestant power.

Towards the end of the century relief acts were passed modifying legislation relating to land, education, residences of bishops and clergy and registration of priests. Catholics were now allowed to teach school, on taking an oath of allegiance to the Crown, and on obtaining a licence from the Anglican bishop of the diocese or his representative.[50] This was 1782.

Another Relief Act was passed in 1792, to give greater force to Catholic demands for political rights, and a Catholic Convention was organized for Dublin in that year. The Convention would probably have been prohibited but it was feared that such action might have sparked off an insurrection. As relations between Britain and France were deteriorating, Westminster was anxious to conciliate Irish opinion by putting pressure on the Irish government to offer concessions. It resulted in the Relief Act of 1793, which did away with most Catholic disabilities. This Act had one

48 Quoted in D. H. Akenson, *The Irish Education Experiment: The National System of Education in the Nineteenth Century* (London: Routledge and Kegan Paul, 1970), 42.

49 Akenson, *The Irish Education Experiment ...*, 42.

50 P. J. Dowling, *A History of Irish Education* (Cork: Mercier Press, 1971), 80.

particular caveat that was not welcomed by the hierarchy. Resulting from the legislation, Catholics could now endow 'a college or university', but it expressly stated that 'any future colleges to be founded should not be for Catholics exclusively, but open both to them and Protestants, and to admit indiscriminately fellows and professors of both religions.'[51] They could bear arms; restrictions on property ownership were removed; all civil and military posts became open to Catholics. Full repeal of the penal statutes did not take place until 1829 with the passing of the Catholic Emancipation Bill.

However, the relief acts of the 1780s and 1790s changed the legal status of Catholicism in Ireland and restored to the Catholic population a measure of social recognition and power unknown to them for almost a century. During the penal era Catholics and Dissenters who taught school were, in fact, flouting the law, but the law was not always enforced. With an increased disposition to religious toleration in the later decades of the eighteenth century, the Catholic Relief Act of 1778 brought some consolation to those who wished to avail of and provide education for Catholics, and this was followed in 1782 by the more important *Act to allow persons professing the Popish religion to teach school in this kingdom ....* [52] James Kelly argues very cogently that traditional interpretations of the Laws are not in line with the endeavours of such repeal legislation. He states that the standard biographies of Nano Nagle, Teresa Mullaly, 'and the studies of diverse religious orders' are at variance with the expressed wishes of the 1782 legislation.[53] Kelly contends that the fact that a Catholic teacher was required to obtain a licence 'from the Protestant ordinary' and should subscribe to the Oath of Allegiance agreed in 1774, reflected the 'reluctance of the Protestant legislature to grant Catholics unconditional relief, but it is necessary to acknowledge that the conditions that were imposed were modest by comparison with the disabilities that were repealed'.[54]

51 Vincent McNally, 'John Thomas Troy, Archbishop of Dublin and the Establishment of St. Patrick's College, Maynooth, 1791–1795', *Catholic Historical Review* lxvii (1981), 568–569.

52 21 and 22 George III, chapter 62.

53 James Kelly, '"I kept my design a profound secret": The Nature and Impact of the Educational Provisions of the Penal Laws', *Archivium Hibernicum* 72 (2019), 346–373; 366.

54 Kelly, 'I kept my design a profound secret', 366.

Many Catholic colleges were established in Ireland as a result of the repeal of sections of the Penal Laws, and the opportunity for Catholics to attend school continued to expand as the legal barriers continued to fall.[55] Furthermore, the 1792 legislation removed the requirement for Catholic teachers to obtain a licence, and in 1795 Maynooth seminary was established. This was a recognition that the toleration of Catholics had come a long way since the early part of the eighteenth century, when the Penal Laws were promulgated. Pitt, under some pressure from Edmund Burke, moved in the direction of offering some concessions to Catholics. Burke tried to gain Catholic emancipation, but this failed, and, likewise with the Catholic franchise, while they were still excluded from parliament.

Reflective Remarks

During this period, education provision stemmed from a number of sources, some theoretically illegal, others belonging to Protestant Societies, and some of these benefiting from state subventions. The hodgepodge nature of this provision cannot be denied.

The early years of the Charter School System were positively anti-Catholic, the following decades displayed a degree of indifference and neglect on the part of the government with regard to its educational concerns. The extensive pay school matrix of popular education which emerged can be seen as being partly in response to the state's formal sense of inertia in the middle years. The popularly titled 'Hedge Schools' provided for the largest numbers of Ireland's schooling-going population in the eighteenth century and well up to the 1830s of the nineteenth.[56]

55 Kelly, 'I kept my design a profound secret', 367.

56 *Report of the Commissioners of the Board of Education in Ireland: Fourteenth Report, view of the chief foundations, with some general remarks, and results of deliberations,* 4. H.C. 1812–1813 (21), vi; reprinted H.C. 1813–1814 (45), v, and H.C. (744), x. Also, see G. Fitzgerald, *Irish Primary Education in the Early Nineteenth Century: An Analysis of the First and Second Reports of the Commissioners of Irish Education Inquiry, 1825–1826* (Dublin: Royal Irish Academy, 2013), 26–38.

The eighteenth century also saw the emergence of a relatively strong force of Protestant education society schools. *The Association for Discountenancing Vice and Promoting the Knowledge and Practice of the Christian Religion*, founded in 1792, 'and originated in a dread of French democracy and infidelity',[57] insisted that the authorized version of the Bible be read by all children attending its schools, and those who taught in its schools were required to be members of the Established Church.[58]

If one subscribes to D. H. Akenson's interpretation the pattern of behaviour that can be unhesitatingly ascribed to the eighteenth-century Irish administration may be depicted in terms of 'colonial mentality'.[59] Akenson maintains that Westminster viewed Ireland as nothing more than a colony, and consequently, particular forms of legislation were not only permissible, but became the norm:

> Legislation initiated in Ireland often dealt with matters untouched by the law in England. Education was one of the areas in which the Irish parliament, with English approval, legislated long before the beginning of the nineteenth century. By the end of the eighteenth century the Irish parliament had aided all levels of schooling, from primary schools to intermediate institutions to university foundations.[60]

One must take issue with Akenson's reference to 'parliament – aided all levels of schooling' as this is not true in relation to the most prolific provider of schooling in both the second half of the eighteenth century and the early decades of the nineteenth – the pay schools (hedge schools). It is safe to assume that the great majority of Catholic children were being educated in these schools, and by the mid-1820s, between 300,000 and 400,000 children were attending such institutions. By the mid-1820s there were approximately 9,000 such schools in the country, the largest, by far of any educational institution.[61] At no stage did the any parliament

57 James Godkin, *A Hand-Book of the Education Question: Education in Ireland; Its History, Institutions, Systems, Statistics, and Progress, from the Earliest Times to the Present* (Dublin: Legare Street Press, 1832), 44.

58 *First Report of the Commissioners of Irish Education Inquiry*, H.C. 1825 (400), 32.

59 D. H. Akenson, *The Irish Education Experiment*, 19.

60 D. H. Akenson, *The Irish Education Experiment*, 20.

61 *First Report of the Commissioners of Irish Education Inquiry*, H.C. 1825 (400), 101–102.

aid these schools. In fact, the state was often suspicious of them, as some of the teachers were associated with agrarian violence.

A Royal Commission of 1834 established that there were 6,436,000 Roman Catholics in Ireland, and that these made up 81 per cent of the total population.[62] There were still some Catholic landowners but, by 1778, the land held by Catholics had been reduced to under 5 per cent.[63]

It was not unusual for both the Irish and English Parliaments of the eighteenth century to debate their obligations to the poor. In England the main concern seemed to be workhouse provision for the destitute and how to treat 'vagrants and vagabonds'.[64] There is hardly any mention of schools in the English House of Commons Journals until towards the end of the century and in Ireland the references prior to 1786 relate to the need to encourage incumbents to provide and maintain schools 'for teaching the English tongue throughout the kingdom' and also to particular charity schools.[65]

Traditionally, the tendency in Ireland was to have state support for many types of schools, including the voluntary 'society' ones, while in Britain, a policy of laissez-faire was dominant, whereby the responsibility for education provision rested with voluntary organizations or philanthropic individuals. 'The less law the more liberty' was the prevailing view.[66] Consequently, England did not have a state-sponsored system of education until forty years later than Ireland's 1831 national system of education.

On a smaller scale, schools did exist in Ireland beginning in Tudor times – parish, diocesan and royal schools, all created by legislation, and endowed through government grants. Another type of school was the Charter School, again receiving state aid. All of these schools were of a

62 Peter Beresford Ellis, *A History of the Irish Working Class* (London: Pluto Press, 1996), 127.

63 Maureen Wall, 'The Age of the Penal laws (1691–1778)', in T. W. Moody and F. X. Martin, eds, *The Course of Irish History* (Cork: Mercier Press, 1996), 220.

64 *Journals of the House of Commons of the Kingdom of Ireland* 23 (1786), 10–12.

65 *Journals of the Irish House of Commons Records,* 22nd day of January, 1799 to the first day of June 1799, 26–33.

66 D. Thomson, *England in the Nineteenth Century* (London: Penguin, 1970), 31.

protestant nature. Hugh Boulter,[67] Protestant Archbishop of Armagh, made the purpose of these schools very clear when he claimed that their function 'was to lead native children away from the Catholic church and into the Established one'.[68] A petition by Boulter, together with clergy of the Established Church and some of the gentry ensured the granting of a charter to one of these voluntary organizations, which was an amalgamation of a number of establishments into the *Incorporated Society in Dublin for Promoting English Protestant Schools in Ireland.* Part of their petition read as follows:

> To the intent thereof that the youth of this kingdom may generally be brought up in the principles of true religion and loyalty in all succeeding generations, we, your majesty's most dutiful and loyal subjects, most humbly beseech your majesty, that out of your great goodness you would be pleased to grant your royal charter for incorporating such persons as your majesty shall think fit, and enabling them to accept of gifts, benefactions and lands to such a value as your majesty shall think to be proper; that the same may be employ'd under such rules and directions as your majesty shall approve of for supporting and maintaining such schools as may be erected in the most necessary places where the children of the poor may be taught gratis.[69]

Parliamentary support was given to the society from 1738, by assigning to the schools of the society the licensing duty levied on hawkers and pedlars. From 1751 an annual grant of £3,500 was given in the first few years which, by 1818, had increased to over £38,000. The grant ceased in 1831.

When we get to Orde's time very few of these schools were working efficiently, and many of them were in such lowly administrative condition that corruption was the fundamental cause.

67 'in him we see epitomised the blending of political and religious outlooks so characteristic of the leaders of church and state at that time'. See K. Milne, 'Irish Charter Schools', *The Irish Journal of Education* 8/1 (1974), 3–29.

68 Referenced in D. H. Akenson, *The Irish Education Experiment,* 30–31.

69 *A humble proposal for obtaining his majesty's royal charter to incorporate a society for promoting Christian knowledge among the poor natives of the kingdom of Ireland* (1730). Quoted in M. G. Jones, *The Charity School Movement, a Study of Eighteenth-Century Puritanism in Action* (London, 1964), 223–228. More recently: Cambridge University Press, 2013.

The importance of one particular benefactor must be mentioned, Erasmus Smith,[70] a Cromwellian soldier who bequeathed funds for the upkeep of schools in his name. In Orde's time, his name was associated with grants to Trinity College, four grammar schools, and over one hundred primary schools (often called English schools, because it was not intended to teach Latin in them). Smith's objective had been to spread Protestantism. 'My end' he claimed 'was to propagate the Protestant faith according to the Scriptures, avoiding all superstition.'[71]

When Orde arrived in Ireland in 1784, he was met with an assortment of schools, established in such an ad hoc manner that they could not be classified as being systematic.

In Parliament, in the 1780s attention was drawn to the condition of the poor in Irish society, the very small farmers, the cottiers, burdened not only by tithe, but by taxes and rent. Many suggestions, by way of alleviation of their plight, were put forward, including exemption from the dreaded hearth tax,[72] the provision of potato plots for labourers, and a drive to substitute beer for whisky. Pitt's suggestion was for a commutation of tithe,[73]

70 Erasmus Smith who died in 1691 was the founder of a number of Protestant schools in Ireland. He was a wealthy merchant and alderman of London. He was what was termed an 'adventurer' and as payment for advancing money to put down the 'Catholic' rebellion of 1641 he was granted £300 in return for his 'adventure'. He was also granted lands in County Tipperary. He had no desire to come and live in Ireland but he had a strong craving to promote the protestant state religion and a keen interest in education. By 1657 he had acquired a considerable landed property in Ireland and he had by title deed made over 13,000 acres in different counties for the formation and endowment of schools in Ireland. See *St. Brendan's Church of Ireland, Tarbert 1814–2014: 200 Years of Change* (Tarbert Historical and Heritage Society, 2014), 57.

71 Quoted in Norman Atkinson, *Irish Education: A History of Educational Institutions* (Dublin: Allen Figgis, 1969), 21.

72 In Ireland, the Hearth Tax was in vogue for the years from 1663 to 1795 and was recorded on Hearth Money Rolls. Only a few copies have survived for some places (mostly Northern Ireland) with most originals destroyed in the 1922 Four Courts fire. The Rolls will list the name of the head of the household and the number of hearths in a dwelling. Also consult the Subsidy Rolls which list the nobility, clergy and laity who paid a grant in aid to the King and Poll Tax Rolls.

73 Tithe was one-tenth of income, in cash or in kind.

but the Chief Secretary, Thomas Orde, advocated a well-planned system of national education.[74] His scheme included a rejuvenated system of parish schools; four 'great schools' modelled on Christ's Hospital, London, providing a high level of vocational education; diocesan schools; two academies, as preparatory schools to the universities, and, possibly, a university in Ulster with its seat at Armagh.

Regardless of whether these societies avowed their proselytizing nature, they were to a greater or lesser extent such. The *London Hibernian Society* (1806) overtly denied proselytism. Yet in a report of 1808, following a deputation to Ireland, it was stated that:

> Popery appears to be exhibited and inculcated there ... with such a decided Partiality in favour of its most fantastic and anti-Christian Features ... nor must it be concealed, that the numeral Predominance of Roman Catholics is itself a prolific Seed of Disunion, not to say political Disaffection. The Hope, therefore, that the Irish will ever be a tranquil and loyal People ... must be built on the anticipated Reduction of Popery.[75]

The Baptist Society (1814) was in the same tradition. It was claimed by the Commissioners to be '... opposed by the Roman Catholic Clergy equally with the *London Hibernian Society*. The principles of both are the same ...[76]

As some of the society schools allowed Catholics to attend, they used the Irish language, not to promote the language, but to advance their particular brand of Christianity. One such society was *The Irish Society for Promoting the Education of the Native Irish through the Medium of their Own Language*. The language was used because '... it was the quickest vehicle for reaching the souls of the peasants'.[77]

The *Society for Promoting the Education of the Poor in Ireland* (1811–1830) was by far the most successful society in educational terms. However,

74 See T. W. Moody and W. E. Vaughan, eds, *A New History of Ireland: Eighteenth-Century Ireland, 1691–1800* vol. IV (Oxford: Oxford University Press, 2009), 283.

75 *First Report of the Commissioners of Irish Education Inquiry*, H.C. 1825 (400), 66.

76 *First Report of the Commissioners of Irish Education Inquiry*, H.C. 1825 (400), 82.

77 See D. H. Akenson, *The Irish Education Experiment ...*, 85.

as it existed well beyond the remit of the current study it is best that we leave it rest here.

Not only in Ireland, but in other countries as well, there was a growing concern about the education of the poor. The idea of popular education emerged in England during the last quarter of the eighteenth century, and experiments in providing for the education of the poor, through the Sunday School Movement, and through the monitorial system, had an influence on Ireland. The growth of this concept of popular education was due to several factors, not all of them altruistic or philanthropic. New political and social ideas were emerging as a result of the French Revolution. In England the clearly demarcated social structures was breaking down and less well-defined social roles were emerging from the expanding industrial age. Problems associated with these changes gave rise to new social needs. The radicalism of the 1790s was a new force in English social and political life. Education became central to radicalism. Locke's earlier views on education and child-rearing were by now fairly common currency in England, and his psychology was an important influence on educational thinking; it was believed that a person's character and behaviour depended on experience, and not on innate ideas. The mind at birth was a *tabula rasa,* an open book to be filled by nurture, and education gained a new power whereby it could bring about social reform, and be used to design and improve the environment of the poor.[78]

Helvétius, like Locke, believed that human beings became what education made them. Such ideas were adopted by the English radical thinkers, who made education central to their policies on social reform, as shown in the writings of Tom Paine's *The Rights of Man* or William Godwin's *Political Justice,* both of which were published within a few years of the start of the French Revolution.

James Mill, utilitarian, taking sides with Helvétius' view of mankind that all are equally susceptible of mental intelligence argued that:

> … the power of education embraces everything between the lowest stage of intellectual and moral rudeness, and the highest state, not only of actual, but of possible

78 David Wardle, *English Popular Education, 1780–1970* (Cambridge: Cambridge University Press, 1970), 2.

> perfection. And if the power of education be so immense, the motive for perfecting it is great beyond expression.[79]

The practical effects of this thinking were seen in experiments such as that of Robert Owen whose newly established infant schools reflected a marked enlightenment, both in their range of curriculum subjects and in methods of teaching. The children were to be governed not by severity, but by kindness, and their learning was to be made as pleasant as possible.

The utilitarian philosophy of the late eighteenth century as exemplified by Jeremy Bentham, among others, placed an emphasis on the utility of education. In England it was believed that if people were educated, they would be less susceptible to the 'delusions and superstitions' which had occasioned such 'dreadful disorders' in France.[80] Adam Smith was of the opinion that an instructed and intelligent people were always more orderly than 'a stupid one' and was in favour of a minimum level of instruction for all.[81] Smith's *Wealth of* Nations (1776) had absorbed one of the tenets of Malthus's *Essay on population,* which in turn received its definitive statement in Ricardo's *Principles of political economy,* which, later, had been re-stated by John Stuart Mill. Each of these commentators was a theoretician. The monitorial schools, however, had little to do with theories, but were a realization of these utilitarian ideas on instruction. The utilitarians were committed to educating the different social classes for their different roles in society, '... the poor to work intelligently and the middle class to govern intelligently'.

James Mill, a utilitarian and leading educationalist, believed that education was of the greatest use for ordinary people, and '... a firm foundation may be laid for a life of mental action, a life of wisdom, and reflection, and ingenuity, even in those by whom the most ordinary labour will fall to be performed'.[82]

79 James Mill, 'Education', *Supplement to the Encyclopaedia Britanica* (London, 1819), 18–19. Cited in John Lawson and Harold Silver, *A Social History of Education in England,* 231.

80 H. C. Barnard, *A History of English Education from 1760* (London: University of London Press, 1966), 45.

81 Adam Smith, *The Wealth of Nations*, 2 vols (London, 1776), 370 (2).

82 Quoted in Lawson and Silver, *A Social History of Education in England,* 231.

The combined forces which gave rise to such interest in education in England had their influence on Ireland and can be seen in the educational developments which took place in the late eighteenth and early nineteenth centuries.

One of the key personalities in stimulating debate on Irish education in the latter decades of the eighteenth century was the Chief Secretary for Ireland, 1784–1787 was Thomas Orde. In presenting a proposed plan of education for Ireland to Parliament, in 1787, he debated on the value of education as an agency of social reform in a way that was in keeping with radical ideas of the day. 'He imputed "all the violent and atrocious acts which had too often disgraced this nation" to a want of education and consequently to a want of obedience to the laws.'[83]

Orde was an active, energetic parliamentarian with many interests other than education. Parliamentary reform was one of these, and when he discussed such an issue with Pitt, he found the prime minister whom he felt was influenced by 'delicacy on the point of consistency', still in favour of parliamentary reform.[84]

Social reform was not an isolated concept, a as being not merely the removal of an evil, as Dr William Drennan expressed when he commented on parliamentary reform as being not merely the removal of an evil, but the 'mines of labour would be opened, and the mists of superstition would dissolve away .... We would all live like Christians, and behave as countrymen.'[85] Others saw parliamentary reform as a prelude to 'great and universal reform' which would include legislative reform, the introduction of state salaries for clergy of all denominations, free trade, the abolition of indirect taxation and the introduction of county courts. The concept of the enfranchisement of Catholics was also raised by two young barristers,

83 D. H. Akenson, *The Irish Education Experiment ...*, 63.

84 Rutland Mss, iii, 148, 157. Cited in F. J. Byrne, W. E. Vaughan, A. Cosgrove, J. R. Hill and D. Ó Cróinín, eds, *A New History of Ireland: Eighteenth-Century Ireland, 1691–1800*, vol. IV (Oxford: Oxford University Press, 2009), 277.

85 William Drennan, *Letters of Orellana* (Dublin, 1785), 40–41. Cited in T. W. Moody and W. E. Vaughan, eds, *A New History of Ireland, IV: Eighteenth-Century Ireland 1691–1800* (Oxford: Oxford University Press, 2009), 268. Drennan was a Belfast intellectual who was a co-founder of the United Irishman. He was Presbyterian.

Peter Burrowes and Todd Jones, who would be active in the 1790s radical movement. Giving more political swagger to Catholics was frowned upon by the Anglicans, and this liberalization would have to wait.

Orde's scheme for education reform was never implemented, but it had the effect of focusing the attention of the government on the question of education in Ireland. He was responsible for initiating several educational investigations during his term of office, and this pattern was continued even after he had resigned.

In the Commissioners' Report of 1791, which was not published until 1857/8, all aspects of the existing educational provisions were criticized. The Act of 28 Henry VIII, which had set up parish schools, was said to be '... defective in making no provision for the education of the children of the poor'.[86] Instead the Act provided that all children were to speak English; that there were to be grants of church lands for schools; and that the schools were to be supported by a tax on the beneficed clergy. The principle object was to increase the use of the English language and so to accomplish a union of the two countries. The Parish Schools depended for their success upon the local incumbent, who often appointed a substitute to administer and organize the school. As there was no general supervision, the efficiency of these schools varied greatly. The total results were small, and these schools failed to achieve the purpose for which they were founded. This failure was due to the weakness of organization and to the greed of the nobility and civil servants. In short, the parish school system was found to be largely non-existent. The clergy had ignored their obligation to provide a school in each parish. It was estimated that there were in Ireland 2,292 parishes, representing 1,100 benefices. Returns were received from 838 benefices and of these, schools were kept in 352. Approximately, 11,000 children were being instructed, and of the benefices co-operating, 201 had schoolhouses. Children paid between one and three shillings a quarter. The master's salary was forty shillings per annum.[87]

86 *Report of the Commissioners of Irish Education Enquiry (1791)*, in *Report of the Commissioners Appointed to Inquire into the Endowments, Funds and Actual Conditions of All Schools Endowed for the Purpose of Education in Ireland*, vol. II, H.C. 1857-8 (2336-I) XXII, Pt. III, 2.

87 *Report of the 1791 Inquiry*, Appendix I, p. 27.

Along with the many shortcomings associated with the parish schools, the 1791 commissioners also found many aspects of the Henry VIII Act wanting. They were of the opinion that the Act which founded the schools in 1537 was inadequate in its provisions and in its objectives. The Act had prescribed the English language as the only subject. Arithmetic, Writing and the principles of Christian religion were ignored. That the person himself had to keep his school and if he failed to find a master he was regarded as being degrading to the order. Furthermore, the salary was too low.[88] The Act's failure could also be laid at the feet of Anglicanism because of its members' heavy opposition to the legislation due to excessive workloads.[89]

These factors caused the Act of 1537 to be a dead letter.[90] At their most flourishing period, in 1810, when there were 549 of them, they represented only about 5 per cent of the total number of schools in operation.[91] As a factor in the system which was built up after 1831 they were of minor importance.

The Charter Schools received a charter from the royal mandate, as The Schools of the Incorporated Society. They began in the first half of the eighteenth century under the leadership of the Protestant Bishop of Cloyne, Dr Henry Maule. These schools were modelled on the English Charity schools. They had a double function; they were used as a bulwark against Catholicism, while simultaneously ensuring social discipline. On the latter of the two, it was, in Midwinter's phrase, a case of 'bless the squire and his relations and keep us in our proper stations'.[92]

The Charity School Movement had begun in England in 1698 with the founding of the *Society for Promoting Christian Knowledge*. The movement

88 *Report of the 1791 Inquiry*, Appendix 1, p. 2.

89 *First Report of the Commissioners of Irish Education Inquiry*, H. C. 1825 (400), xii.1., p. 3.

90 William Jacques, *The Chief Factors Determining the Developments in Primary Education, Ireland, 1831–1947* (Unpublished Doctoral Thesis, Queen's University, Belfast, 1952), ch. 1.

91 G. Locker Lampson, *A Consideration of the State of Ireland in the Nineteenth Century* (London: A. Constable, 1907), 125.

92 Eric Midwinter, *Nineteenth-Century Education* (London: Longman Group, 1970), 19.

spread rapidly and was parish-based. By 1750 there were over 2,000 such schools in England dealing with more than 50,000 children. In addition to religious instruction, these children were taught reading, writing and arithmetic, while some of these schools taught sewing, knitting, spinning, ploughing and gardening. These children were prepared for domestic duties, factory work and labourers.

In Ireland the earliest Charity School was opened in the Dublin Liberties in St. Patrick's Cathedral in 1704. The forty or so pupils 'were supported for several years by the private contributions of a few charitable persons'.[93] The objectives of the Charity Schools were that, the children of the poor might be decently clothed and usefully educated, being taught to read, write, and cast accompts, and instructed in the knowledge and practice of the Christian religion, as professed and taught by the Established Church. By the late 1720s financial difficulties began to emerge, and it was soon recognized that a wider trawl would have to be made to gain greater financial support. About 1730 a campaign for charity schools brought pressure on the government 'for obtaining his majesty's royal charter, to incorporate a society for promoting Christian knowledge among the poor natives'.[94] Charity schools had been one of the mechanisms of maintaining Protestant interest in Ireland, and these schools had been encouraged by the Protestant interest, and Catholics were almost obliged to educated their children as Protestants and to prevent 'occasional conformity' by Catholic converts.[95]

Hayton argues that the charity schools did not for the most part seek to spread Protestantism among the native Catholics. Instead (not as much as

93 *Methods of erecting, supporting, and governing charity-schools, with an account of the charity-schools in Ireland, and some observations thereon.* Pamphlet in King's Inns Library, Dublin (Dublin, 1721). Reproduced in T. Corcoran, *State Policy in Irish Education, 1536–1816*, 99.

94 John Richardson, *A Short History of the attempts that have been made to convert the popish natives of Ireland, to the establish'd religion: With a proposal for their conversion* (London, 1712; republished by Creative Media Partners, 2018). Cited in D. W. Hayton, *The Anglo-Irish Experience, 1680–1730: Religion, Identity and Patriotism* (Woodbridge: Boydell Press, 2012).

95 See D. W. Hayton, *The Anglo-Irish Experience ...*, 117.

the later Charter schools) they gave their attention to the weaker brethren in the Protestant community.[96] Most schools, Hayton claims, were expected to enrol Protestant children before Catholics, and, then but only then to enrol Catholic children if the Protestant supply had dried up:

> The function of the earliest schools (charity) had been to recall poor Protestant children to their religion and to instil in them the virtues of hard work and obedience, while the conversion of Catholics was left to the implementation of laws and the working of self-interest, bolstered by individual persuasion and pious example.[97]

The theology of the Church of Ireland disposed its members to pay more attention to the spiritual welfare of their young Protestant members than that of the recalcitrant Catholics. In other words, they were more concerned with saving the souls of 'fellow Protestants and in doing so avert an adverse judgment of Providence'.[98] However, popery did not wither, but survived to flourish again.[99]

This happened when Maule and Hugh Boulter gained a royal charter which was granted in 1733. This royal charter meant that the Charity schools would become 'Charter' Schools. One thousand pounds a year came from the King, along with large parliamentary grants. By the time we get to Orde's time the grants had increased to eleven and twelve thousand pounds a year.

However, abuses abounded, including malnutrition, floggings, lack of clothing, chronic ill-health and lack of hygiene. These schools began with Protestant and Catholic children, but latterly, it was mostly Catholic children who were attending. The children's education was frequently neglected, and it seems the local committees had no control over what was happening in the schools. In the words of K. Milne:

> Whether through incapacity, indifference, or sheer lack of inclination, the Society found these committees to be far from assiduous in their duties. Again and again reports reached Dublin of masters who were flouting the Society's rules in one way or another .... Not all cases of irregularity escaped detection, abuses were discovered

96 D. W. Hayton, *The Anglo-Irish Experience ...,* 153–154.

97 D. W. Hayton, *The Anglo-Irish Experience,* 171.

98 Hayton, 173.

99 Hayton, 149.

> and masters dismissed. But the Society was badly served by the local committees who failed to see, if they did not positively ignore, the cruelties and negligence that eventually came to light under public scrutiny ... Without strict and vigilant supervision the system invited abuse and got it in large measure.[100]

The Charter Schools were most severely deprecated. It was reported that:

> ... in most of the said establishments the instruction, cleanliness, and health of the children had been most grossly neglected; that they had not been allowed sufficient food, clothing, or other necessaries; that in many of these schools they are half starved, half naked, and covered with cutaneous disorders, the effects of filth and negligence, while in some of those the children of the masters and mistresses appear fresh, clean and in good health.[101]

In their concluding remarks, the Commissioners observed that none of the schools on public foundation, charter schools, parish schools, royal or diocesan schools had answered the intentions of their founders, and that with few exceptions they had been of little use to the public.

Thomas Orde would have been familiar with Charter School problems, as he was acquainted with John Howard. Also, as Atkinson claims, 'quite apart from low efficiency, it is clear that Charter School education had proved to be exceedingly expensive, partly through speculation and wasteful administration.'[102]

To compound all the other negative reports on the Charter Schools, Jeremiah Fitzpatrick, Inspector of Prisons, visited twenty-eight Charter Schools in 1786–1787. According to him, the children were barbarously treated by their masters, and were 'puny, filthy, ill-clothed, without linen, indecent to look upon .... The schoolrooms were dilapidated and dirty, though the private apartments of the masters and mistresses were comfortable.'[103] A similar account is given in the Hely-Hutchinson report of 1791:

> That in most of the said establishments the instruction, cleanliness, and health of the children had been most grossly neglected; ... that in many of these schools they are half

100 K. Milne, 'The Irish Charter Schools', *Irish Educational Studies* 4/1 (1984), 48–49.
101 *Report of the Commissioners of Irish Education Enquiry (1791) ...*, 17.
102 N. Atkinson, *Irish Education*, 26.
103 See James Godkin, *Education in Ireland*, 33.

> starved, half naked, and covered with cutaneous disorders … while in some of those the children of the masters and mistresses appear fresh, clean and in good health.[104]

Fitzpatrick's condemnation of the secular features of the charter schools was candid and all-embracing:

> … that … many of them afflicted with Itch, Scald &c. and that Athleticity, so strongly marked in the Children of the Poor in this Kingdom, however shabby their Clothing, is not to be found in Charter Schools, which he attributes in a great measure to the nature of their employments, the bad quality of their food, to confinement, and to the effects of wholesome exhalations from filthy bed-clothes and foetid straw inclosed [sic] in odiously besmeared Tickens. He says the nature of their labours injures the health of many who sit carding and spinning at the Linen Wheels; the Attitudes cripple their limbs, whilst the constant discharge of saliva to wet the Thread injures their digestion; and employed at the large wheels, their limbs being yet in a grisly state, they contract the habit of turning in their knees and toes, and otherwise become distorted, which follow from the positions into which they are thrown, which even at the state of Manhood speaks their early employments; and by the master's paying for the children's labour he becomes more interested in the profits arising from it than in their making the wished progress either in a proper knowledge of the principles of religion or education. He also states that the Charter School lands are in general in worse condition than their neighbouring grounds …[105]

In one particular school, in Newmarket, where the master had a cotton manufactury supplied by the linen board received very unfavourable reports in 1786, including one from Sir Jeremiah Fitzpatrick. It appears that there were six boys and nine girls in the establishment, and twenty-four boys and thirteen girls apprenticed to it from other locations and schools. One of the complaints was concerned with the fact that the apprentices were not receiving any education, and only wore shoes and stockings on Sunday while attending church. This is just another example of the corruption that went on within the Charter School System. In the reports

104 Cited in T. Corcoran, *State Policy in Irish Education,* 179. This report suggests that of the forty-four establishments under review 'not more than five or six were properly taken care of'.

105 Schedule annexed to *Report on Protestant Charter schools,* dccccxx. Quoted in Oliver MacDonagh, *The Inspector General: Sir Jeremiah Fitzpatrick and the Politics of Social Reform, 1783–1802* (London: Croom Helm, 1981), 91–92.

there are many occasions highlighted where masters were drawing down a salary for no appreciable level of teaching taking place.[106] Milne draws attention to the relevance of the likes of Jeremiah Fitzpatrick in his reports on the schools, and even though the Incorporated Society appeared to make efforts to deal with the problems in its schools, the tone of Fitzpatrick's reports leaves no room for doubt about the ineffectiveness of these attempts.[107] In short, Fitzpatrick condemned the masters and mistresses, who were 'more interested in the profits arising from it than in promoting either religion or education'.[108]

The Commissioners' Report of 1791 related primarily to parochial schools, the proposals made seem remarkable for their time. It was, of course, the era of relaxation and civil rights were being recognized at home and abroad. The penal laws were being modified, Catholics could enjoy equal civil and religious rights. It was the time of the radical and utilitarian movements, when the right of 'all' to receive education as a powerful social agency was recognized. These ideas and beliefs were reflected within the pages of the 1791 Report. Education was no longer seen as the prerogative of the privileged few, and the Report also recognized religious freedom for Catholics; '… it is our opinion that the children of Roman Catholics and Protestants should be admitted indiscriminately into the schools …'[109] Thus the right of all classes to avail of education was conceded.

The system of education put forward was a multi-denominational one, in which the needs of different creeds were recognized with regard to religious instruction. They recommended that the clergy of each persuasion should attend each school for the purpose of religious education. Thus a process was set in motion whereby a system of national education could be established in Ireland.

The Report also recommended the removal of the control of parish schools from the local Protestant vicar and place it in the hands of lay

106 See Kenneth Milne, *The Irish Charter Schools 1730–1830* (Dublin: Four Courts Press, 1997), 162–165.

107 Milne, 179.

108 Milne, 196.

109 *Report of the Commissioners of Irish education Enquiry (1791)* …, 3.

managers including Roman Catholics.[110] Though, the 1791 Report encompassed the bulk of the criteria for such a system, it was another forty years before such a scheme was introduced in Ireland.

On a positive note, he was an innovationist when it came to education provision, and though his plans were not implemented during his own time, he had the foresight to understand the importance of legislation in education provision. This concept of legislation was abandoned when the national system of education was established in 1831. Perhaps, at this juncture, it might be opportune to put forward Orde's earlier plan of 1786.

The Plan of 1786 and Conclusion

In April 1786, Thomas Orde made an announcement in the Irish House of Commons in College Green, Dublin to the effect that resolutions he had in mind were worth discussing in parliament. He proceeded to address the House:

> Upon a subject of very high concern to the nation – the improvement of the education of youth. The object of his resolutions was to extend the means of education universally through the country at so cheap a rate that few persons should be excluded from its advantages.[111]

Through the interest expressed by the Provost, Thomas Orde, who was in Ireland for a relatively short period of time, and engaged in a very onerous and demanding task as Chief Secretary. The job at hand was made all the more exacting because of the political situation in Ireland, the so-called

110 Burton, Edward F., 'Richard Lovell Edgeworth's Education Bill of 1799: A Missing Chapter in the History of Irish Education', *The Irish Journal of Education* xiii/1 (1979), 24–33, 25. See also, Lyons, Tony, *The Education Work of Richard Lovell Edgeworth, Irish Educator and Inventor, 1744–1817* (New York: Mellen Press, 2003).

111 *The Parliamentary Register: Or, History of the Proceedings and Debates of the House of Commons of Ireland* vol. V1, 447.

'independence of Grattan's Parliament' and the unrest among, not just the Catholic majority, but also disaffected members of the Protestant community. Coupled with that was the unrest in France, both before and following the revolution, and the threat this posed to Great Britain. It was a time of unease, society was in something of a turmoil, change was afoot, the industrial age had much sway in the manner in which society was progressing. For Orde, his time in Ireland made few concessions by way of allowing for the advancement of proposals on education provision. Orde had a difficult self-inflicted charge in hand. It was fortunate for him that a man like Hely-Hutchinson was like-minded in many respects.

Through his investigations, and by way of his association with the Provost, Orde was in a position to be aware of much of the problems associated with Irish education. For instance, he knew of 'several endowed schools throughout the kingdom, and some of them rich, but their very opulence was the chief cause that defeated the intention of their founders'.[112] In his plans, he addressed the issue of corruption within the management of these schools.

He continually stressed the importance of education for Ireland; a universal national system, with a legislative foundation was uppermost on his mind. In the House, he:

> moved that the national foundation of one or more public schools, with regulations adapted to, for facilitating and extending to the youth of this kingdom the means of good education, would be of great public utility.[113]

The above quotation from the parliamentary debates in the Irish House of Commons in April 1786 indicates to the reader that Hely-Hutchinson's *Outlines of a Great Plan* with a critical analysis at state and endowed schools and his comments therein did not fall on deaf ears when it came to Orde. As a result, Orde was not in favour of continuing with the practice of endowing the masters of these schools, as they had displayed indifference towards their charges for many years. He:

112 *The Parliamentary Register*, vol. VI, 447.
113 *The Parliamentary Register*, vol. VI, 448.

> rather hoped some method might be adopted to help or support young people under a course of education, not merely by paying the master, but by assisting the scholars in the pursuit of knowledge, and afterwards, to encourage scholars so formed to become teachers, rising in succession.[114]

He had done some calculations and surmised that the expense would be relatively small in comparison with the benefits that would accrue to the nation.[115]

Orde's motion was seconded by Hely-Hutchinson who agreed very strongly with the motion. He could not wish for more:

> than to see a wise and well adapted plan for extending the advantages of a good education to the youth of this country carried into effect, and at the same time that he was persuaded such a plan might be put into practice at a small expense; he was also convinced that it was extremely wanted. And that infinite advantage would accrue to the kingdom from it.[116]

It was the turn of Mr. Corry, representing the Borough of Newry, to speak:

> The intention of the right honourable gentleman deserves the highest praise from every person, and, if it was not a subject of very great magnitude indeed, I should not hesitate to confide it implicitly to the right honourable gentleman who seconded him. But I do not fully understand the subject, and cannot avoid thinking the mode of proceeding somewhat odd. Perhaps it is a wise one; but as it is not clear to me, I beg the right honourable gentleman will descend to the level of my comprehension, and have the goodness to explain it.[117]

Orde's response was that he felt it was sufficiently plain, reiterating that the principle of his plan was necessary for the nation, as it would improve the circumstances of the youth of Ireland. He assured the House that if the plans had been finalized, he would have proceeded in a different manner and not defer to the following session of Parliament a business of such magnitude. That ended the discussion on Orde's input regarding

114 *The Parliamentary Register*, vol. VI, 447.
115 *Parliamentary Register*, 447.
116 *Parliamentary Register*, 447.
117 *Parliamentary Register*, 448.

the topic of education. Mr Corry, then took the floor with a question on trade with Portugal.

Later, in the same parliamentary session (6 April 1786) Mr Corry returned to the topic of education when he asked Mr Orde about the possibility of presenting 'an humble address' to the Lord Lieutenant, requesting that his Grace will be pleased to give directions for the preparing plans[sic] of the necessary arrangements for establishing public schools, with an estimate of the expense:

It was then ordered, that the proper persons do make returns to the House of schools of Royal or other foundations in the respective dioceses in this kingdom ... the names of the masters and assistants, the salaries or allowances paid to the masters, ushers, assistants, or other officers belonging to the said schools, as the same stood on the 25th day of March, 1786, together with the number of scholars at that time in each school respectively, distinguishing the free scholars, the boarders and the day scholars. It was also ordered that the registers of the several dioceses be returned to the House, on the first day of the next session, an account of the English schools kept by the rectors or vicars in their respective dioceses, with the number of scholars therein on the 5th day of March, 1786. This collection of statistical material from the existing Protestant/English schools in Ireland, at both primary and higher levels, formed the fulcrum points about which Orde designed his lavish education plans for Ireland.

It should be recognized that Orde's innovative plans for Irish education bore testimony to a mind that was open and liberated to inclusivity in an age when such a concept was hardly part of the body politic. However, there is one aspect of Orde's plan which excluded the majority of people in Ireland – the Catholics. Did he think that by degrees the Catholic families would send their children to his 'Protestant' schools? This is a topic we will endeavour to tackle at a later time.

Many have said that Orde's efforts in the 1780s were a 'touchstone' upon which was built the remarkable number of investigations and reports that we witness over the next half-century. For setting this train of events in motion, Orde must be recognized, and though Orde is more or less lost to history, he is still worthy of inclusion as a valued contributor to the history of education in Ireland. His plan for a system brought the day nearer when a system would eventually be put in place. We should grant the final word in this chapter to a certain D. H. Akenson when he remarked that Orde left an educational legacy behind that continued in progress and influence long after he had resigned as Chief Secretary.

CHAPTER 3

Orde's Education Plan Revealed: April 1787

Introduction

We have seen to what degree Thomas Orde may have been influenced by Hely-Hutchinson's outline of different plans for certain aspects of Irish education. We have also seen how Orde took on board a strong commitment to reforming education in Ireland. Firstly, he undertook an investigation into the contemporary state of education, and then he proceeded to embark on a detailed plan to subdue what was inefficient by rooting out the dismal and the bleak aspects, and replacing these with an education system, backed by the legislature, which would answer the social and intellectual needs of Irish families.

Hely-Hutchinson suggested to Orde that it would be advantageous to have an inventory of the endowed and state-sponsored schools in Ireland. At the close of 1785, the Chief Secretary, Orde, wrote in the margins of proposals for a scheme of education sent to him by the Provost, Hely-Hutchinson, who had suggested the Charter Schools should be investigated, 'This should really be attended to.'[1] Orde was also concerned about the Royal and Diocesan schools. As early as April 1786 he requested that the Irish House of Commons in College Green should order that returns be acquired about the schools in question and detailing their various types and their pedagogical aspirations. Orde was eager to have this done, and he had pre-empted what the Provost had in mind, and had already begun the process of investigation. During 1786, he had made contact with various

1 See D. H. Akenson, *The Irish Education Experiment*, 69.

members of the Anglican Hierarchy to establish the number and status of schools which were operating under the auspices of the Crown.[2]

Orde wished for more than reform of Irish education; in his mind a reconstitution of all the tiers was in the offing; his vast array of statistical information which he had received from the church bodies, coupled with the interest Hely-Hutchinson, John Howard and Jeremiah Fitzpatrick had expressed in the process of intervention in education provision in Ireland acted as a catalyst for Orde and his endeavours. Howard found time to visit Charter Schools in 1782, 1784, 1787 and 1788, but why? Was it because his acute nose for administrative frailties might unearth something dastardly. Visiting schools, for him, was not that difficult as he traversed the countryside as part of his job as prison reformer. In a correspondence with Samuel Whitbread in 1787 Howard left no doubt about the Charter Schools in Whitbread's antenna:

> I was with Mr. Orde this morning. He with the Provost has taken the charter schools under parliamentary consideration. In this country every public institution is a private emolument; all are corrupt or totally inattentive, from the highest to the lowest.[3]

In all areas of planning and writing reports so as others can act upon them, it is essential to take upon oneself a thorough exploration of the vicissitudes therein. So, with Orde, who gathered as much information as he could on the schools[4] in Ireland, that were initiated by the state or endowed by organizations, such as Societies. In such situations, one quality of enormous importance is note-taking, and Orde was a prolific note-taker and letter-writer, both of which were very useful when building up a dossier on different types of schools in Ireland. This chapter addresses Orde's keen preparatory work before his speech in the House of Commons; his plan of April 1787 is dealt with in considerable detail,

2 See Bolton Manuscripts, Ms. 15887 (1).

3 J. Field, *The Life of John Howard with Comments on His Character and Philanthropic Labours* (London: Longman, Brown, Green Longmans, 1850), 142. See Reprint, published by Fb&c Limited, 2018.

4 He was not interested in schools of a Catholic nature. His chief interest in education had to do with its provision was through the auspices of the Established Church (Anglican or Church of Ireland).

analysing his treatment of the parish schools, the provincial schools, the Diocesan Schools and classical education, the Collegiate schools, a College of Visitors (inspectors) and a second university. The chapter ends with reflective comments and concluding remarks.

Keen Preparatory Work

He was wont to see certain 'experts' in the field of education in order to ascertain their views on a particular issue. For example, with regard to a Mr John Cooper, secretary to the Erasmus Smith Charity, Orde had written in his notebook: 'Ask old Cooper ... about them and particularly of surplus undisposed of.'[5] He also intended tracking down a Mr Wolfe who apparently could provide him with information regarding Ballyroan.[6] Mr Gibbons, secretary to the Incorporated Society would be useful with information on the Charter Schools. In all these notes (he had two full notebooks) we witness Orde preparing for his final plan, and to be announced in the Irish House of Commons when the time was appropriate and opportune.

The more information he gathered the more he realized the situation regarding Irish education was in a dreadful state. He reflected on the plight of what lay before him before he came to a final plan that would be accepted by the Commons in Ireland, and be effective as an antidote to the existing circumstances as well as being ameliorative with the introduction of new schools of varying types. He deplored the state of the Charter Schools, and found they were 'of little use'.[7]

5 See Bolton Manuscripts, Ms. 15,887 (2). See C. McElroy's thesis, *Thomas Orde, 1746–1807 ...*, 58.

6 See Bolton Manuscripts, Ms. 15,887 (5). John Wolfe, M.P. for Kildare. See McElroy's thesis, 58n.

7 Bolton Manuscripts, Ms. 15,887 (1). He was informed of this by a Mr Lloyd in a letter dated 2 April 1786. Similar information was available from John Wesley and John Howard. Following his tour of Ireland in 1783, Howard had had a meeting with Hely-Hutchinson who undoubtedly passed on his impressions to Orde. See C. McElroy, *Thomas Orde 1746–1807 ...*, 59.

Sir Jeremiah Fitzpatrick, inspector general of prisons, reported to Orde in 1787 on 'the shameful conduct of several charter schoolmasters,[8] and their ignorance was condemned by the commissioners in 1791.[9] The Royal Schools also caused him immediate concern, as did the possibility of a second university.[10] Orde's original notes, though haphazard in nature and lacking coherence, indicate his strong desire to aid the education process. To that end, his was willing to listen to others, some of whom had greater understanding of the situation than he. For example, Mr Edward Tighe M.P. for Wicklow.[11] He was quite willing to take change in a piecemeal manner and recognizing that the state's purse strings were not inexhaustible. Perhaps, this level of realism stemmed from the reactions he received back following requests he had made. Take, for example, the reply he received from Bishop William Beresford of Ossory was quite terse and direct: 'Upon the most minute enquiry, I find that there is no school of royal foundation in the diocese of Ossory.'[12]

It should be worth apprising ourselves at this point of what James Kelly has to say on the matter of the information collected by Orde:

> Most of what was collected was distinctly unflattering and reports in the public papers that endowed schools had been converted into 'shameful sinecures', that Enniskillen School, which had land worth £1, 200 p.a., had scarcely a pupil, that Raphoe worth £600 had none, and Armagh worth £700 had but a 'few boys', fuelled the demands for action. Additional impetus was provided by the growing realisation that the ills which prevailed in the endowed schools were prevalent in all areas of education, [and] that the parish clergy were as likely to pocket the money as to provide schools and, above all, by the fact that the charter schools which were held in such esteem by protestants but were currently under unofficial investigation by Jeremiah Fitzpatrick and John Wesley, were in 'wretched state'.[13]

8 Bolton Manuscripts, Ms. 15,881.

9 *Report of the Commissioners of Irish Education Inquiry, 1791.* Not published until 1857–1858 (2336), xxii, vol. 11, pt. 111, 358.

10 Bolton Manuscripts, Ms. 15,887 (10).

11 Bolton Manuscripts, Ms. 15,887 (9). Notes here relate to Parish, Charter and Diocesan Schools as well as the foundations at Kilkenny, Ballyroan and the Blue Coat Hospital, Dublin. See McElroy, 59.

12 Bolton Manuscripts, Ms. 15,881 (2).

13 In James Kelly, 'The Context and Course of Thomas Orde's Plan of Education of 1787', *The Irish Journal of Education* 20/1 (1986), 3–26.

Orde understood education to be of benefit for the individual, but he also saw it as being useful in social terms within the wider community. Certain advantages would accrue from a sound education system and he felt that it could give 'a new turn and direction to the national character and habits'.[14]

Applying this to Ireland, he found a great want of education and the time was ripe to extinguish 'the disgraceful stigma with the balsam of prevention'.[15] He was particularly keen on protecting society from various types of law breakers, and, to this end, he felt a good, effective education system would, at least, enable the perpetrators be aware of the consequences of their criminality. Education would:

> make the wretches sensible that they compel the stroke .... That they not only incur the certainty of punishment, but wantonly throw away blessings by their wildness and indocility .... Let them have instilled into their minds some little notion of the compact and the duties of society; make them comprehend in some degree the comforts as well as the restraints of civilisation; the extent of their instruction may after all even thus be included in the simplest maxims of right and wrong.[16]

For Orde, education was an *instrumentum regnum* and as such it could, if used in a particular manner, control the masses. However, there seems to be a contradiction in his thinking, if this is true, because on the other hand he wished for a saving of the masses through education. On many occasions, he expressed his desire to improve the lot of the Irish people, especially those on the lowest rungs of society.[17] To this end, he spoke in positive terms about the intrinsic value of the peasantry in Ireland:

> I am moved that they have been suffered to remain as a rich metal in the mine, which no fashioning hand of an artist has hitherto attempted to polish into beauty, and upon which no stamp of instruction has been set to give it an acknowledged worth and currency.[18]

14 J. Giffard, *Mr. Orde's Plan of an Improved System of Education in Ireland*, 12.
15 J. Giffard, *Mr. Orde's Plan ...*, 13.
16 J. Giffard, *Mr. Orde's Plan ...*, 14. It is unlikely that the criminal class, especially those of a recidivist nature, would benefit from lessons on 'right and wrong'.
17 However, he had no place in his plan for the inclusion of Catholic Ireland.
18 J. Giffard, *Mr. Orde's Plan ...*, 15.

Orde, in his speech in College Green, laid before his audience of MPs a strategy for Irish education which was unprecedented in its range all-enveloping nature. He said:

> The system, which I would propose, should be extended in its benefits to all parts of the community. It should begin with the lowest ranks of the people, and ascend in different gradations to the highest, and tend to qualify the youth of each order for excellence in the stations and pursuits belonging to each. It may do more. It may give to the youth of every class an opportunity of bringing out and improving talents, with which nature may have endowed them, fitted to a rank superior to that which fortune had allotted to them. The preservation no less than the immediate increase [sic] of learning may thus be ensured by the formation of more able instructors to future generations. It must be of material consequences to establish the uniformity and steadiness of sound discipline throughout the whole system.[19]

It may not be an exaggeration to suggest that education for Orde was a universal cure or elixir for all ills of humankind. He was fearful that his efforts in Ireland might be viewed as a means of depressing the Irish spirit, but he was quick to point out that learning had never yet made humans degenerate into servility.[20] For him, all ranks in society were 'ennobled by the lessons of virtue'.[21] He argued that learning had made a contribution to every nation, and the bravest people whose history could be traced combined undaunted courage with the love and cultivation of letters. Even in Sparta, 'the community ... asserted their rights in that respect [the provision of educational] as superior to those of parental authority. The children were accounted the offspring of the public, and the nurture of their minds was secured by a public provision.'[22]

It seemed to the Chief Secretary that there was a role for government in the process of education, in so far as:

> The general superintending power of government must encourage and enforce the full execution of every trust in every department. I think it right to declare that this plan is not of course designed to interfere with the progress of many schools already

19 Mr Orde's Speech, 25–26.

20 See McElroy, 62.

21 J. Giffard, *Mr. Orde's Plan ...*, 15.

22 J. Giffard, *Mr. Orde's Plan*, 23.

> established, or to preclude the institution of others at the will of liberal individuals, who may be disposed to form them; but it may in many instances afford an example, worthy of imitation both in the modes of instruction, the rules of discipline, and the care of inspection.[23]

Ireland, it seemed to Orde, was in need of something similar in which the Irish needed to be rescued 'from a state of being confounded with the brutes of the forest'.[24] They must be taught about the privileges and prerogatives of humanity, and make them sensible of its dignity and instruct them … 'that morals, truth, industry, honesty and peaceableness [sic] are the ornaments of it'.[25]

Referring to the endowed schools, and their 'shameful neglect' he felt that 'somewhere along the way the intentions of the original founders of these institutions had been lost'.[26] Regarding teachers in his proposed scheme, Orde felt that teachers should be remunerated according to their exertions,[27] and emulation should be the motivating factor for both teachers and scholars. And, so as to encourage the 'exertions' of the teacher, he felt that he should be provided with a fixed salary, but, in addition to it, payment would be made on the basis of how many pupils he was teaching. This, of course, encouraged the teacher to teach as many pupils as he could, and if he could develop the school as a recognized establishment within educational circles, all the better for his pocket.[28]

Funding for the scheme would have to be established, and his proposal:

> was to alter the charges which heretofore had been imposed indiscriminately on the beneficed clergy. He suggested that an allowance of forty shillings per annum be fixed on all livings of £100 a year and up to £150. All livings from £150 and up to £200 should pay sixty shillings. And for all livings above £200 a year, he suggested

23 Mr Orde's Speech, 26.

24 J. Giffard, *Mr. Orde's Plan …*, 19.

25 J. Giffard, *Mr. Orde's Plan …*, 20.

26 See McElroy, 63.

27 This was an early attempt at Payment by Results.

28 This policy by Orde was almost a century ahead of the official Payment by Results introduced in England in 1862 and in Ireland in 1871 (partially), but extended nationally in Ireland (1872). It was abandoned in 1900, and replaced by the Revised Programme.

> an annual increase by what he termed 'a sort of poundage on the excess' of sixpence in the pound. He believed there should be a similar contribution, in like proportion from the proprietors of rectoral and impropriate tithes.[29]

Any further financial needs might be offset by contributions from the more prosperous proprietors within the parish whom Orde felt would be happy to help out their poorer fellow-parishioners. In such a fashion, then, a reasonable standard of living might be provided for a well-qualified and efficient teacher.

If there is one word from the English language for which Orde had a particular *penchant,* it is the word 'emulation'. In case the monies collected as described above provided a surplus, he had plans for this. In order to encourage students through reward, he organized prizes and exhibitions for all levels within his scheme. There were prizes for well-behaved, diligent children, who might get a present of clothes, or, perhaps, a free meal. Meritocracy played a large part in Orde's thought processes, and he would have all the children striving to do their best at everything, and to outdo each other.

Though Orde had designed a scheme which provided for the teacher's salary, there was still one aspect that caused some concern. The teacher's place of residence had to be supplied by the parish, but it was unlikely that the parish could fund such an enterprise. To that end, Orde hit upon the idea of a parliamentary grant, and costed the total amount per annum of £5,000. An alternative would be using some of the monies in the Erasmus Smith Charity Funds. There was always a reliance on private benefactors who might supply a house along with an acre of land, so as the teacher could be more or less self-sufficient.

Parish schools should open on Sundays, for catechism and devotional activities, he believed, for the children of the Established Church, and also for those children from other denominations who were engaged in manual work on weekdays and could not attend school. The Established Church was not entirely happy with Orde's proposals as its leading church men saw the proposals as a 'diminution in the Church of Ireland's control of schools

29 C. McElroy, *Thomas Orde, 1746–1807 ...*, 66–67.

and an increase in "rational" teaching and the inculcation of "the principles of rectitude and beneficence into the hearts of the rising generation"'.[30]

In order to ensure what he had proposed had been put into practice, it was necessary to form an inspectorate to oversee the whole system. This, he said, would be the responsibility of the Protestant minister in the parish, who would have first-hand knowledge of the conduct of the teacher and the good order of the school. Church-wardens would also act as visitors by checking up on attendance levels and cleanliness. Reports would then be dispatched to the Established Church bishop, who would keep a register of all schools in his diocese. Orde hoped that the bishops themselves would visit and make 'strict and serious enquiry into the state and management of the school in every respect'.[31] There is, however, very little evidence in his plan that indicates he had a broad concept of school inspection. Essentially, his definition of an inspector is someone who judges upon appearances, with much less emphasis on pedagogical substance. His 'inspector' deals with the teacher and his administrative skills more than his teaching prowess, which is at the kernel of the teaching and learning process.

However, Orde must be commended for his efforts in portraying a very vigilant approach to the schools he had in mind. He even had plans in which the local magistrate would make visits to the schools, and he went so far as to suggest that circuit judges might collect all the reports on school matters before eventual presentation to the Lord Lieutenant. Part of his plan to thoroughly oversee the work of the parish schools was in the amalgamation of the governors of the Erasmus Smith Charity for English Schools and those of the Incorporated Society for Protestant Charter Schools.

In England during this period, and because of a laissez-faire state policy, there was no equivalent parish school as a state-sponsored concept. Instead, there were Dame Schools, often compared to 'baby-minding

30 J. Fitzpatrick, *An Essay on Gaol-Abuses, and on the Means of Redressing Them: Together with the General Method of Treating Disorders to Which Prisoners are Most Incident* (Dublin: Byrne and Brown, 1784), 94.

31 J. Giffard, *Mr. Orde's Plan ...*, 41.

establishments'.[32] There were other types of primary schools in England. The charity school movement began with the founding of the Society for Promoting Christian Knowledge in 1698. Another type was the Industrial School whose aim was to teach reading and writing but also to train the children:

> In industrial occupations such as spinning, printing and sewing and also in such employments as gardening, cobbling and carpentry .... These schools, however, gradually disappeared since they could not compete with the new factory developments in which children proved a valuable resource of secondary income to parents, as well as cheap labour for the employers.[33]

Going back to Orde, it is interesting to point out now that he included some of the industrial subjects in his schools, which we will examine later.

The Sunday School movement was begun by Robert Raikes in 1780, and this expanded rapidly to become a sort of nationwide popular education scheme. It had a religious leaning which was an attribute of Orde's plans for Ireland in 1787.[34] Orde's proposals of 1787 dealt with a concept which had no meaning in his own country – the state endowed or sponsored school.

Beginning with the lowest tier, Orde felt that each tier would produce scholars of 'rank superior to that which fortune had allotted to them'.[35] Great care should be undertaken when drawing up a curriculum, as different schools required different curricula. His scheme had no place for the arbitrary whims of individual teachers, and to this end, he emphasized the need for an inspectorate.

Though Orde often referred to all religious persuasions attending school together, he also recognized that 'Catholics will not send their children to English Protestant Schools'.[36] Access for Catholics to education in the eighteenth century was mainly through the pay schools, more

32 Ivor Morrish, *Education Since 1800* (London: Allen and Unwin, 1970), 4. Morrish also exonerates some dame schools from the historians' disparagement. See pages 4–5.

33 Morrish, 6.

34 Orde was simply siding with contemporary Anglican thought.

35 J. Giffard, *Mr. Orde's Plan ...*, 25.

36 Bolton Manuscripts, Ms. 16,360.

popularly known as hedge schools. Though a fee was required to attend hedge schools, the people were still willing to support these schools instead of the endowed schools, many of which did not charge a fee. It is impossible to ascertain a reliable or accurate figure for hedge school attendance in the eighteenth century, but a *Report on the present state of Popery* of 1731 puts the figure at 549 schools. The next set of figures made available come from the *First Report of the Commissioners of Irish Education Inquiry* based on 1824 statistics, and the figure attending the hedge schools was somewhere between 300,000 and 400,000.[37] This is not entirely reliable either as some of institutions may have been overlooked. It is probably safe to assume that, during Orde's time, up to 300,000 children attended hedge schools. The number of pay schools operating in Ireland at this time has been recorded as 9,000.

Orde 'identified education as a means of "attaching the Roman Catholics and of making their leaders in some degree dependent upon government."'[38] Kelly qualifies this statement by referring to Orde's strategy of obliging prospective Catholic clerics to be educated either in the College of Dublin (TCD) or in some other 'acceptable institution', to oblige them to take 'an oath of allegiance', and to obtain 'licences to officiate'.[39] It is very unlikely that this was ever going to be a successful outcome. The intransigence of the Roman Catholic Hierarchy would not allow any of its clerics attend what was perceived to be a Protestant institution. In any case, Orde maintained that children educated in the schools he was promoting should be brought up in the established religion. The staffing in these institutions would also be Established Church controlled. If Catholic children attended these institutions he held out to them what he termed an 'excellent opportunity'. There would not be any form of compulsory attendance for Catholic children.

The two notebooks in which Orde drafted his proposals contain the following notes:[40]

37 *First Report of the Commissioners of Irish Education Inquiry*, H.C. 1825 (400), 101–102.

38 J. Kelly, 'The Context and Course of Thomas Orde's Plan of Education of 1787', 12.

39 Bolton Manuscripts, Ms. 16,369, 7, 1–2. See J. Kelly, 'The Context and Course of Thomas Orde's Plan ...', 12.

40 Bolton Manuscripts, Ms. 16,380, 8–9.

> *Parish Schools*
>
> Whether in many cases the houses provided for charter schools might not be applied to these purposes upon alteration of the establishment for charter schools.[41]
>
> *Provincial Schools*
>
> Reasons why the charter schools could not be of so much utility in their former footing as by this improvement.
>
> Objects of these, in addition to those of the charter schools, to better formation of the national manners and a juster [sic] direction to industry and ingenuity.

Orde's notes identify lack of supervision as a crucial element in the neglect of the parish schools. It was up to the Anglican bishops, he announced, to set a good example, but:

> The visitations of the bishops in Ireland are not like those in England, by a regular circuit through the several parishes of the diocese. The visitation here is only an assemblage of the parochial clergy at the bishop's palace, where he enquires about all matters – to their cures and belongings. It must therefore be hoped that the bishops will continue some method by which they may receive exact information which may be depended upon.[42]

Orde was very obviously calling for a more streamlined approach by the bishops, whereby they could be so informed as to be in a position to pass judgement on the processes of schooling in their respective dioceses. His notes also indicate that the days of the charter schools are numbered. He had in mind an alternative utility for the buildings in use as charter schools .... 'If the establishment of charter schools should be dissolved, the houses provided for them in many places might be allotted to the purpose of parish schools',[43] and then he proposes the funding allocated to the charter schools be re-deployed towards the education of girls.

41 See Appendix.

42 Ms. Top. Ireland. D.2, p. 14. Cited in K. Milne, *The Irish Charter Schools 1730–1830*, 206.

43 Ms. Top. Ireland, 19. Cited in K. Milne ..., 206.

Orde's Plan of 1787

In the introductory portion of his speech to the assembled members of the Irish House of Commons in College Green, 12 April 1787 Orde appears to be almost apologetic for what he is about to propose. On the subject of education, he stated:

> Confidence indeed however can hardly be withheld, even without such invitation to it, upon a subject where there can be no call or object for the official interference of government, and no possible motive for its exertion of a forward zeal, but the ambition (which is directly avowed) to obtain possibly a deserving place in your remembrance, and thereby at the same time to testify the high rate of estimation at which such distinction is valued. No symptom or suspicion of parties or division among us can be apprehended upon a question of such interesting importance to the whole community, and which is brought forward upon this simple footing, to excite the attention and engage the co-operation of every friend to his country.[44]

That sounds like a very reasonable early introduction to his stock of education proposals. His speech took three hours to deliver, and at no stage did anything dogmatic or arbitrary emerge from its contents. The conservativism of his plan was conspicuous, though sprinkled here and there with liberal snippets. As McManus illustrates, 'it was clear ... that he belonged to the conservative school of thought which urged the use of education for the pacification of Ireland.'[45] Here was an individual who came to Ireland to hold high office as Chief Secretary to the Lord Lieutenant (who also took up his post in 1784), and who within a short period of time, following observations and conversations, made a decision, without any official obligation to do so, that the best he could offer to the Irish people was an education system which they did not possess. And, this system was for 'all' of the people, irrespective of colour or creed. However, there were caveats and sideshows, concerns which will be teased out within the ensuing pages.

44 Mr Orde's Speech, 9–10.

45 Antonia McManus, *The Irish Hedge School and Its Books, 1695–1831* (Dublin: Four Courts Press, 2002), 38.

In general terms, education was becoming a serious contender as one of the major social issues of the eighteenth century. This was true of both England and Ireland. As far as Ireland was concerned, education could prove to be the ideal vehicle by which the 'hearts and minds' of the troublesome Irish could be won over. An Irish race educated in elementary fundamentals, assimilated culturally with England and without nationalistic or identity aspirations would be of economic assistance to the Empire from the later stages of the eighteenth century onwards during which extended trading and industrial revolutions dominated the economic horizons. With that in mind, Orde's plan of 1787 fitted in very neatly with the prevailing mindset among parliamentarians on both sides of the Irish Sea. The plan was a forerunner of what was to come in 1831, namely, the 'direct violence' which had dominated relations during the seventeenth and eighteenth centuries would now be replaced by 'indirect methods' which ignored the background, culture, language, history and ethnicity of the people of Ireland.

The argument that Ireland, as a colony, could be used as an experimental location for social legislation that might not be tolerated in England where laissez-faire political and economic policies were more rigid is a little simplistic. It can be argued that education was but one of a series of social policies such as an organized police force, improved health services and a Board of Works that were introduced in the 1830s. Orde, in the 1780s, was instrumental in re-organizing a police force for both Dublin and the rest of the country. It seems that there are parallels between Orde's contribution to government of the country and those individuals of the 1830s, but not solely confined to the education sphere.

Strong animosities, suspicions and hatred existed between the main religious denominations within Ireland and the Established Church. Although the Established Church was a minority denomination within a predominantly Catholic society argued that it had a special position and a right to government support in promoting Protestantism. The Catholic Church, emerging from a century of repression, felt it should get financial support for educating the poverty-stricken masses of children. The Presbyterians, who like the Catholics had suffered under the Penal Laws, also sought direct state support for their tradition.[46] Thomas Orde's plan was one such intervention to counteract the wishes of the dissident churches such as the Catholics and Presbyterians. His plan, on a multi-denominational or mixed basis, simply arranged for all creeds to be educated together in the same classroom. While Orde's plan never got to the implementation stage, the Stanley and Wyse national school system introduced many years later (1831) mirrored that of Orde.

Orde, with such a mass of information under his belt, proceeded to write a plan, beginning in late 1786 and continuing up to April 1787. The plan had been fomenting for some time, and it was now time, once the gestation period was over, to package the plan in the shape of fourteen resolutions and place them before the House of Commons in College Green.

In 1787, the Irish Chief Secretary presented the Irish parliament on the 12 April with a scheme for a five-tier educational system, encompassing parish, provincial, diocesan and collegiate schools, and two universities. By any stretch of the imagination this was a cultured, urbane, refined, advanced and complex approach to a revitalization of Irish education. By the time he stood in the House of Commons on 12 April 1787, Orde still had some finer points of his plan to negotiate, but other than that, he had enough fodder with which to cast his audience into an awe-inspiring gasp of approval.

Orde's Plan for Rejuvenating Parish Schools

Immediately prior to outlining his plans for each individual education tier Orde excused the long-winded introductory aspect to his speech in the House of Commons. At this point, he also took the opportunity to reiterate the importance of a newly revamped education system which should bring 'relief and improvement' to the people and he expressed the

46 See a full exposition of these ideas in Eamon Harvey, *The Origins and Development of the National School System, 1831–1880* (Unpublished M.A. thesis submitted to the University of Ulster (Magee), 1993), 16–19.

view that this new system would, through 'proper instruction' point out the consequences to both individuals but also:

> to the mass of the nation, and to the state itself; and above all to exhibit, in proofs of reason and illustration, the superior advantages which would be likely to result from a general reformation, and the establishment of a general system: I shall seek to compensate your kind indulgence and attention, by as much brevity in what remains for me to say, as may be consistent with a due perspicuity.[47]

The parish Schools were the brainchild of Henry VIII, and by the Act of 28 each parish was obliged to teach any child who presented for instruction, in the English language:

> The English language at the time of enacting the law was as little known to the peasantry of Ireland as the language of Athens or Rome, and therefore teaching children to read was not a very trivial duty. Yet, though every parish minister is bound by oath to comply with this act, the only thing done towards carrying it into effect is, a commutation of 40s. per annum paid by the minister in each parish.[48]

The policy of anglicization is palpable in this Tudor legislation, but when we reach Orde's era, these parish schools were practically non-existent. The original Henrician legislation was to enable English cultural, religious, social, and political interests to advance in Ireland, and education was one of the mechanisms by which this could be done. The parish schools had failed to accomplish these ambitious objectives 'and that they were unlikely ever to achieve them because of the inadequate number of schools, low numbers of pupils, and the Catholic perception that they were little more than glorified proselytising agencies'.[49] It was Orde's wish to breathe new life into the Act of Henry VIII, and under the auspices of the Established Church replenish what had never seriously matured in the first instance. In some instances the Established Church ministers were providing the sum of forty shillings in each parish for the upkeep of the schools. However, there was little or no accountability as the nature

47 Mr Orde's Speech, 28–29.

48 *Parliamentary Register,* vol. 6, 489.

49 James Kelly, 'The Context and Course of Thomas Orde's Plan of Education of 1787', *The Irish Journal of Education* 20/1 (1986), 3–26.

of the whole business was arbitrary. The whole approach was nothing short of a Protestant crusade, with, hopefully tacit Catholic compliance and implied Presbyterian deference.

In his speech in the Irish House of Commons Orde exhorts the efforts of Henry VIII, and upon examining that policy Orde comments that:

> we shall find that there was something of policy as well as of charity in the institution of parish schools under that reign; however, of most excellent tendency, and worthy of being perpetuated. The more general knowledge and use of the English language were certainly then, if not the sole, at least the principal objects of parliamentary concern, in directing the introduction of these schools ...[50]

He found that the whole business of this legislation was woefully inadequate, and his knowledge of these parish schools suggested that 'which is called reading English is, I fear, little more than the articulation of certain sounds perfectly unincumbered without any regard to meaning'.[51] For him, the entire business was haphazard and lacking in co-ordination. And, despite its widening to include the whole country by the late seventeenth century, it never catered for more than 11,000 pupils.[52] The fact that in the 1780s only 361 parish schools were in existence, and these were meant to cater for a population of four millions which further illustrates the extent of the failure. The existing scheme often left the teacher in a parish, scrounging about for scholars to attend his school; this smacked too much of trying his chance, but without any support from the parish community. Sectarian issues often played a role in creating obstacles for the teacher – forty shillings was 'no inducement to the master to risk his safety, and perhaps his life in a Catholic parish'.[53] Orde had evidence where parishioners had not allowed a Protestant school master keep a school, and there were also difficulties for teachers in finding accommodation

50 John Giffard, *Mr. Orde's Plan of an Improved System of Education in Ireland, Submitted to the House of Commons, 12 April 1787, with the Debate Which Arose Thereon* (Dublin, 1787), 30–31.

51 J. Giffard, *Mr. Orde's Plan ...*, 31.

52 Colm McElroy, 'Thomas Orde and Educational Innovation, 1786–1787', *Irish Educational Studies* 15/Spring (1996), 152–163, 154.

53 Bolton Manuscripts, Ms. 16,360.

in some parishes; and there were instances where bishops had appointed Catholic teachers, there being no Protestant available or willing to teach in the school.[54] Kenneth Milne may well be correct when he alludes to the difficulties finding Protestant teachers. In quoting Orde he exclaims that in some places 'it is difficult to prevail upon a protestant to attempt the instruction of children for fear of being starved or knocked on the head by the Catholics'.[55]

Orde had stipulated that the choice of teacher should be undertaken with great care, especially in respect of morals and propriety of conduct. He must be 'indispensably a Protestant, but Catholic children should be admitted to the school'.[56] There is no doubt about the proselytizing nature of Orde's plan. He also stipulated that apart from teaching the three Rs the teacher should be able to inculcate the principles of honesty, truth and industry. And, in a general comment he exclaimed that:

> All ranks, all descriptions of society, are amended and ennobled by the lessons of virtue; and where morals are defective, the taint of vice corrupts and defiles the Patrician still more than the Peasant. Where has been the Nation, to which learning has contributed no advantage? What people has not been rendered more formidable by knowledge as auxiliary to their bravery? Has public liberty been injured by understanding its true meaning? Has freedom lost its exertion, because society has learned to comprehend and to obey the law?[57]

He presented his credentials in the Irish House of Commons without ambiguity and he clearly outlined, in a long speech, each of the divisions he had in mind for the new system of education. Beginning with the lowest level, the parish schools, he had the following remarks to make:

> The first object … which presents itself to notice, in surveying the different divisions of this system, is the scheme by which the lowest and most numerous order of the community have within their reach such moderate advantages of instruction and

54 Bolton Manuscripts, Ms. 16,360.

55 Bodleian Library, Ms. Top. Ireland d.2, 11–12. See K. Milne, *The Irish Charter Schools 1730–1830* (Dublin: Four Courts Press, 1997), 102.

56 Bolton Manuscripts, Ms. 16,360. Also, see Mr Orde's speech in the Irish House of Commons, 33.

57 Mr Orde's Speech, 15–16.

> precept as may make them at once more happy and more useful members of the society. This object has in some degree already heretofore engaged the attention of the legislature by an act, which is still in force and observance, although the provisions of it do not go to form a sufficient establishment in these days; nor is the nature of the obligation under it such as in itself to secure the gratuitous communication of instruction to the poor, which I would wish to recommend in the strongest manner.[58]

Orde then, continues with his speech and makes an observation about 28 Henry VIII's 1537 legislation for Parish Schools. In considering the real motives of the Act, 'we shall find that there was something of policy as well as of charity in the institution of parish schools under that reign; a policy, however, of most excellent tendency, and worthy of being perpetuated.'[59]

He concludes the part of his speech dealing with parish schools, announcing that about nine hundred parishes in the country 'in which these establishments may be usefully formed' but then he qualifies this by stating 'that in many of these parishes, particularly within great towns or cities, there are already sufficient accommodations and conveniences for the schoolmasters and children, and that in such of course it will not be requisite to incur the expence[sic] of providing these arrangements. And if there are different circumstances from parish to parish, local input should decide what is best for local requirements, and 'the numbers can always be augmented according to the encreased [sic] population or the proper demand of the districts'.[60]

> He was very concerned about the circumstances in which the parish schoolmaster found himself. He witnessed many defects within the parish schools and in particular 'it is evident that the provision which is made at present for the school-masters, is not an adequate inducement to a man of sufficient qualifications for such an employment; and in recommending a fund therefore to be provided for the gratuitous instruction of a certain number of children in each parish, I must of course be supposed to represent the necessity of a decent maintenance and protection to the school-master.'[61]

58 *Mr. Orde's Plan of an Improved System of Education in Ireland.* His speech in the Irish House of Commons, 12 April 1787, 30.

59 Orde's Speech, 30.

60 Orde's Speech, 43, 41–43.

61 Mr Orde's Speech, 33.

And, he added the following:

> It may not be an unwise regulation to secure and encourage the exertions of the master, that even in providing a fixed salary for him, a part of it, or an addition to it should be paid to him with each scholar, whom he shall be directed to teach.[62]

This is not the only occasion when Orde referred to a dual payment system for teachers. He was seventy-five years ahead of the introduction of Payment by Results in England and eighty-five years ahead of its adoption in Ireland. Payment for the teachers should be sourced from a number of locations: it had been exclusively laid at the feet of the beneficed Protestant clergy, but this did not fare very well and was 'without distinction;' other persons should be introduced at this stage. He suggested a tax to be imposed on certain persons, but left it to his audience in the Commons to deliberate upon the details.[63] He did, however, put forward a rule-of-thumb figure of forty shillings per annum for the schoolmaster, but that, he said, would be the 'lowest rate of contribution'.

Orde never tackled the ins and outs of methodology, nor did he submit a detailed curriculum that his proposed schools should follow. He did however, insist than in reading, as a school subject, the teacher must ensure that the child understands what is being read. The following is how Orde expressed this wish: '... I should hope that in teaching the children to read, it should be an essential part of the master's duty to engage their understanding, as well as their tongues in the performance of their lessons.'[64] This was unusual at the time, and it was not until the mid-nineteenth century, and later, that critics began to emerge regarding the lack of emphasis on the child's comprehension of what was being read. Charles Dickens and Mathew Arnold were strongly vociferous in this regard. It came to a head during the results era in the second half of the nineteenth century, reading was split into 'Heads' and 'Sub-heads': the 'Heads' counted for teacher payment, but did not address the child's understanding, while 'Sub-heads' did address comprehension, but did not count for payment.

62 Mr Orde's Speech, 34.
63 Mr Orde's Speech, 34–35.
64 Mr Orde's Speech, 40.

In the eighteenth century, word soundings sufficed for reading, with little emphasis on meaning – Locke, in the seventeenth century had his dice to aid reading, while Rousseau later, placed an emphasis on desire to read; each had positive aspects, but word soundings on their own had little or no merit. Lawrence puts it very well when she exclaims that:

> Reading must not be taught mechanically. Children must learn to read with understanding and with natural expression, not to 'roar, and sing out what they read'. The schoolmaster should consider it his duty to teach the pupils to read with understanding, and carefully to observe whether they know the meaning and import of the words they utter. This they can never do, if they are not taught to read distinctly, and as nearly as possible in the tone of conversation.[65]

And, acquiring the art of reading:

> Will be useless, if the teacher has confined his instruction to the mere sounds of words, especially where these sounds are very different from those which we are accustomed to use in conversing with each other.[66]

During Orde's speech in the House of Commons, College Green his sense of democracy came to the fore, and one example of this referred to the ages at which children should attend the revamped parish schools. He suggested five or six years as a starting point, and they should stay for about six years. However, he was not dogmatic about this, and he allowed the MPs the opportunity to ruminate while they made a decision. In a similar vein, he did not insist on visitors calling to the schools to inspect, but was willing to allow democracy take its place in a final decision regarding school inspection, and who should do it.

At various times throughout his preparations for his speech, and within his speech, Orde refers to the situation that children from all walks of life would be welcome in the schools he was proposing, and, then on page

65 E. Lawrence, *The Origins and Growth of Modern Education* (Baltimore: Penguin Books, 1970), 212. Lawrence is quoting Elizabeth Hamilton, *Cottagers of Glenburnie* (Palala Press, 2015; 1st edn 1808).

66 Hamilton, 369. Lawrence, 213.

forty-five of his published speech he states that the children attending should be 'brought up in the established religion'.

Four Great Provincial Schools

Following on from the parish schools Orde envisaged what he termed provincial schools in which, once the basics had been taught in the parish schools, there would be a concentration on developing each boy's skills and knowledge in his own particular field of interest. Ireland did not possess schools of this type and Orde modelled them on Christ's Hospital in London. The curriculum in such schools could include reading and grammar, geography, writing and accounts, navigation, modern languages, trade, manufacturing mathematics, geometry, architecture, drawing, husbandry and agriculture.[67] This was a curriculum that resembled what was taking place in the Industrial Schools in England.

Orde's plan proposed the formation of 'four institutions of four schools, or hospitals, or academies: one of them in each province of this kingdom'.[68] And:

> In each of these schools a certain number of children shall be gratuitously lodged, boarded, cloathed[sic] and instructed in those studies, which may be most suitable to their pursuit of such future occupation, as may be the object of their choice, or of their particular talents and abilities. These academies are designed to form and to send into active employment, besides those who can be engaged only in manual labour or subordinate stations of life.[69]

Every step of the way was to be underpinned by legislation, with His Majesty as patron, the Lord Lieutenant and the united corporations as acting guardians and governors, with a president, whose province and

67 C. McElroy, 'Thomas Orde and Educational Innovation, 1786–1787', *Irish Educational Studies* 15/Spring (1996), 152–163. See Mr Orde's Speech, 54–55.

68 Mr Orde's Speech, 46.

69 Mr Orde's Speech, 46–47.

powers will of course be properly defined and settled.[70] The rules for the nomination and admission of students must be ascertained in the statutes; the period of their admission may be properly fixed at between 7 years of age and 10 and their continuance should end not later than sixteen.

His plan with Provincial Schools as described by him would be 'of great utility to a class of the people not so numerous as the former, but perhaps the most interesting to the community at large'.[71] His objective in having these types of schools was:

> to educate ... an useful order of citizens in different gradations, for the exercise of various occupations in several lines of active business. This idea can hardly be said to be founded on the model of any present establishment in this kingdom, although something of the kind upon an inferior footing may be traced in the Blue-coat Hospital of Dublin. But these schools are intended in fact to become by degrees an improved substitution for the present charter-schools. And the excellent institution of Christ Hospital in London, suggested to me the general principles of the proposed foundations.[72]

He says he does not wish to denigrate the charter schools, and he does not suspect that the charter schools have been neglected, but:

> they cannot, from the nature of them, so scattered in situation, so liable to escape notice and proper observation, and so limited in their objects, produce the advantages, of which a more decided system of higher aim might be rendered capable.[73]

Orde stipulates in his speech in College Green that the purpose of these Provincial Schools, in so far has he can contemplate, should serve the needs of the kingdom of Ireland in the 'formation of national manners' and of 'just direction to national industry and ingenuity'.[74]

Orde never rested on his laurels, and he was keen to commence on these four schools immediately, the first location he had in mind was at New

70 Mr Orde's Speech, 47.
71 Mr Orde's Speech, 43.
72 Mr Orde's Speech, 43.
73 Mr Orde's Speech, 44.
74 See Mr Orde's Speech, 44.

Geneva[75] in Waterford. He did some costings, and the entire school would consist of eight or nine hundred scholars at a cost of £12,000 per annum.

He also entertained the idea that girls could also attend the provincial schools, though with a modified curriculum, embracing reading, writing, grammar, arithmetic (for both sexes), and spinning, knitting, needlework, embroidery, lace-making, millinery, mantua-making, pattern drawing and housekeeping for girls. He had in mind four separate provincial schools for girls, each catering for eight hundred scholars (with six hundred coming from the Charter Schools). This was a highly innovative initiative at the end of the eighteenth century. Orde has to be commended. In his notebook 'On Education', he had written:

> A certain small number of girls might also be made partakers of the benefit of such institutions though in a separate establishment to be rendered more proficient in the exercise of those occupations to which women are best suited.[76]

In his speech Orde refers to the separate accommodation for female students:

> ... whose residence might possibly have been so arranged, as to have been kept separate from that of the boys, and yet have been within reach of the advantage of the general superintendence and protection.[77]

Though both church and state in England 'recognised that a certain proportion of the male population had to be educated in secondary schools ... girls were not included'.[78] In some middle class instances, home education

75 New Geneva was a colony created in Waterford for disaffected citizens (Calvinists) of Geneva following the short-lived Geneva Revolution of 1782. Built near Passage East, the colony was commissioned by the Irish Parliament and approved by the Crown. However, the Genevans abandoned their plans to settle in Waterford, the site became a military barracks instead. During the Rising of 1798 the barracks was used as a holding centre for captured *United Irishmen* rebels, many of whom were executed, transported or conscripted. Today, the only remains of New Geneva are its ruined walls in a grassy field.

76 Bolton Manuscripts, Ms. 16,360.

77 Mr Orde's Speech, 58.

78 N. Hans, *New Trends in Education in the Eighteenth Century* (London: Routledge and Kegan Paul, 1966, 1st edn 1951), 194.

was thought to be suitable for girls. Other than that some availed of private boarding schools, but these only came into existence in the second half of the eighteenth century.[79] It is, therefore, not an exaggeration to claim that Thomas Orde's plan for female education can be seen to be ahead its time.

The Chief Secretary, in his notes stipulated that these provincial schools were meant 'to be an improved substitute for Protestant Charter Schools'.[80] He was quite astute in attempting to inveigle the remaining Charter Schools, who were members of the Incorporated Society, into supporting this measure which would increase the amount of charitable instruction they were engaged in. It was his plan that the new Incorporated Society would have responsibility for the Provincial Schools along with the remaining Charter Schools.[81]

The objective of these schools was to provide the opportunity for Protestant students to cultivate their interests and once the basics had been achieved the school then concentrated on the curriculum as outlined above. All the clientele would be brought up in the Protestant faith. The intake to the schools would be divided into 'first division' and 'second division', the second having three times the number of scholars as the first. Those admitted to the first division would be recommended by 'certain privileged persons'. The second tier would cater for those who were currently admitted under Charter School protocols. This meant that Catholic students were excluded apart from an interlude from 1775–1803.[82] This reference is, of course, in connection with the existing Charter Schools.

It is very likely that, unless a 'privileged' person recommended a young student for entry to these schools, the chances of a Catholic getting onto the 'First Division' were very slim indeed. Theory is one thing, but in practice, with 'privilege' persons being mainly from a middle class Protestant background, Catholics doing well in these schools could have been a rarity. Orde

79 See Hans, Chapter X, 194–208.

80 Bolton Manuscripts, Ms. 16,360.

81 See McElroy, *Thomas Orde, 1746–1807 ...*, 71.

82 D. H. Akenson, *The Irish Education Experiment*, 33. See *Report from the Commissioners of the Board of Education in Ireland; Third Report, the Protestant Charter Schools*, 19.

even stated in his notes that …. 'Preference … of admission … to children born of Protestant parents'.[83] James Kelly, writing in 1986, copper fastens the protestant nature of the Provincial Schools when he says:

> As with the parish schools, the role of the provincial schools was clearly defined. They were to provide predominantly middle-ranking protestant children with the qualifications necessary to allow them become mariners, mechanics, farmers, surveyors, and architects.[84]

The two divisions were to be kept apart within the confines of the school, with distinct provision to be made for separate instruction, diet, clothing and lodging.[85] This was tantamount to having two separate schools under one roof. Orde had planned that the age of admission to these schools would be somewhere between seven and ten, and they would not stay beyond sixteen.

Orde's plan was to have one guardian or principal in charge of the entire school; he was supported by a headmaster who had responsibility for all the instruction taking place on the premises; each subject area would have its own specialist teacher or undermaster. Orde envisaged some flexibility within the school, that is, movement between the two divisions, but then he stated quite categorically that 'these higher classes will be reserved for the boys of the first division'.[86] It would appear, therefore, that only those children who were sponsored by a 'privileged person' could manage to gain access to the First Division, and, thereby benefit from it, while the second division students may have been apprenticed to whatever occupation they had been studying for.

The curriculum in the Provincial Schools was weighted heavily in favour of vocationalism, and especially with regard to industry and trade. However, Orde had provision made within the campus of the Provincial School for a 'classical school', in case a student wished to abandon the practical-type or applied curriculum and venture forth into classical

83 Bolton Manuscripts, Ms. 16,360.

84 J. Kelly, 'The Context and Course of Thomas Orde's Plan of Education of 1787', *The Irish Journal of Education* 20/1 (1986), 3–26, 13.

85 McElroy, …, 72.

86 Bolton Manuscripts, Ms. 15,888, 49.

studies.[87] Here, students would stay until eighteen or nineteen, and then they could present for exhibitions to university.

Orde had New Geneva in Waterford in mind for the first Provincial School, and the students for this school:

> Should be drafted from the several Charter Schools, with regard to their superiority of talents and good behaviour, and by this means indeed an improvement might be formed in such of the Charter Schools as should remain, if the object of removal of the children from them to this higher situation should become a spur to emulation and industry.[88]

These draftees would not make up the total provincial school student population as some space had to be kept for those recommended by 'certain privileged persons'. It crossed Orde's mind that two instead of four Provincial Schools might do if the emulation engendered in the existing Charter School children increased the standards all round. He felt the New Geneva should serve Munster and Leinster, while another for Connacht and Ulster could be organized.

Coming closer to his Common's speech in College Green, Orde was still uncertain about how many provincial schools he should plan for. Allied to that was another issue, the location at New Geneva may not become available as a building in which to have a school.[89]

Funding, as always, can be a problem for ventures like Orde's. He did, however, have access to the annual Charter School sponsorship of approximately £13,000, topped up with a government grant of £7,000. He was also

87 If classical education should be introduced, a proper endowment shall be obtained of a school for the learned languages here to qualify boys for the university and to support them with exhibitions here during a certain number of years .... Recommend also in the mode of instruction to depart in some degree from old habits and to delay attention to the learned languages to a more advanced age than usual and to devote more time and pains to a thorough foundation and knowledge in English Grammar and the use of the English language in writing, declaiming, etc., ... Boys found unqualified for learned education to be placed after trial in one of the other classes or schools. From Bolton Manuscripts, Ms. 16,360. Cited by C. McElroy, *Thomas Orde, 1746–1807 ...*, 74n, 60.

88 J. Giffard, *Mr. Orde's Plan ...*, 56.

89 Bolton Manuscripts, Ms. 16,360.

hopeful that generous individuals of a 'charitable and patriotic disposition' would contribute.[90] He also felt that 'every well-endowed Corporations within the province might reasonably make an annual contribution and have power of nomination'.[91]

As we have observed, Orde was very faithful to 'emulation' in educational development and with regard to that he felt that school visitors (inspectors) should have discretion in choosing two or three parish school pupils and then nominating them to the Provincial Schools.

The grammar schools of England formed the prototype for Orde's 'great schools' or 'academies' or 'provincial schools'. The top grammar schools in England were sometimes referred to as 'great schools'.[92] These schools were generally Anglican, and attained a humanist hue and one commentator suggests that their origin owes most to John Colet and his statutes for St. Paul's in 1518 which 'provided for humanist studies in Greek as well as Latin'.[93] When we come to Orde we find that the humanist slant does not readily find a place in his heart as his provincial schools emphasize technical arts, navigation, mercantile knowledge, agriculture, modern languages, and so forth.[94] However, as the eighteenth century progressed Grammar Schools began to make changes to their curricula, including alongside the classics such topics as commercial subjects. This change was forced upon them as they began to compete with a growing number of private schools. Another major shift in policy was in the second half of the eighteenth century when more fee-paying middle class pupils were taken on board. An example of such a school was Christ's Hospital, London.[95] This school did not confine itself to studying the classics but it had a number of other divisions as well. In addition to schools that allied themselves to the classics (for those entering university or the Church), there was also

90 J. Giffard, *Mr. Orde's Plan …*, 59.

91 Bolton Manuscripts, Ms. 16,360. Cited in McElroy, *Thomas Orde, 1746–1807 …*, 77.

92 S. J. Curtis, *History of Education in Great Britain* (London: London University Tutorial Press, 1950), 112–114.

93 M. Sanderson, *Education, Economic Change and Society in England 1780–1870* (London: The McMillan Press, 1983).

94 D. H. Akenson, *The Irish Education Experiment*, 64.

95 C. McElroy, *Thomas Orde, 1746–1807*, 78.

a school boys who prepared boys for the navy; a writing school was also available for those entering trade or business, and a reading aspect to it for those who could not read upon entering the school.

Apart from Public Schools and Grammar Schools, England also had quite a cosmopolitan and cultured arrangement of Dissenting Academies. These combined theology and science, and occasionally the classics:

> The Academies introduced secular subjects and openly trained for all professions. The Church monopoly of classical education was frequently infringed by Dissenters, who kept many classical schools for long periods.[96]

Without Church control, these academies had the freedom to make changes at their own behest, and as a result they were able to develop into well-organized institutions, while experimenting with different subjects, and new methods.

The Dissenting Academies, in an overall sense, dealt with the study of mathematics and the various sciences more so than the Grammar Schools. The academies also pioneered business education, and one of the best-known Dissenting Academy, Warrington, ran a three-year course for commercial students, 'combining science, languages, book-keeping, geography and trade subjects'.[97]

It is difficult to avoid a comparison between Orde's plan for Provincial Schools and the philosophy of the Dissenting Academies throughout England. And, not only the Dissenting Academies, but another institution embodied in the concept of the Private Academy which emerged in England during the eighteenth century. These institutions provided a broad range of subjects, including Literacy, Mathematics and the Sciences, Vocational and Technical subjects, as well as Accomplishments and Physical Training. For example, under Vocational and Technical we find the following subject areas – Military Science, Engineering, Navigation, Shipbuilding, Architecture and Merchants' Accounts as well as other Commercial subjects, and Agriculture in some instances.[98] The curriculum provided

96 N. Hans, *New Trends in Education in the Eighteenth Century*, 59.

97 M. Sanderson, *Education, Economic Change and Society in England, 1780–1870* (London: The Macmillan Press, 1983), 25.

98 Nicholas Hans, *New Trends in Education in the Eighteenth Century*, 65.

by the Private Academies became associated with a combination of liberal education and technical instruction. And, was the case with Orde's Provincial Schools, the Private Academies in England divided individual institutions into 'Schools', such as Naval Schools, Commercial Schools, Grammar Schools, and so forth. These academies catered for the lower middle classes in which the fees were moderate and poor students with proven ability were trained without charge.[99]

The Chief Secretary outlines what he thinks is of great importance in learning the various sciences:

> In regard to the study of the different sciences, which are recommended, it will, I am confident, appear to you to be right, that we should provide not only for instruction in the theory of them, but in practice and experiment also______ Proper space, therefore, and apparatus, and practical assistance, should be gradually prepared for the execution of this essential object.[100]

Orde's knowledge of education provision in England is very clearly prominent, and reflected in his plans for Irish education as elucidated in his speech in the Irish House of Commons, 12 April 1787. To the extent that Orde's familiarity with education provision in England coloured his own ideas for education provision in Ireland, it stands to reason, as Colm McElroy claims, that Orde 'did not work in a vacuum'.[101]

His classification for parts one and two were indicated in his speech in the Irish House of Commons, in which he spoke of:

> ... the two first of them should embrace the people in the lowest degree, and in the degree next above it; both of which I should thereby hope to lead forward to the chance of an advanced gradation.[102]

Orde also addressed the issue of female education as he exclaimed:

99 C. McElroy, *Thomas Orde, 1746–1807*, 80.
100 Thomas Orde, *Mr. Orde's Plan of an improved System of Education in Ireland*, 51–52.
101 C. McElroy, *Thomas Orde, 1746–1807*, 80.
102 Thomas Orde, *Mr. Orde's Plan of an Improved System of Education in Ireland*, Speech in the Irish House of Commons, College Green, 12 April 1787, 29.

> I have hitherto spoken only of a partial plan in favour of one sex; but I should be sorry not to be supposed to have given my attention to a provision of some advantages in education to the other sex also, who might be brought up in a manner to be rendered more proficient in the exercise of those occupations, which women are competent and well suited to; reading, writing, grammar, arithmetic, spinning, knitting, needlework, embroidery, lace-making, millinery, mantua making, housekeeping, drawing, &c. &c.[103]

It is a pity Orde did not complete the list. This statement does, however, indicated that female education was worthy of a place in his grand plan, albeit not an equal place at the table, by any means.

In his notebook 'On Education' Orde offers another input to female education:

> A certain small number of girls might also be made partakers of the benefit of such institutions though in a separate establishment to be rendered more proficient in the exercise of those occupations to which women are best suited ... are studies and occupations more adapted to women and in which the improvement of skills might be of much greater utility.[104]

He did not view women and their rights as individuals or groups on a par with their male counterparts. He did, however, offer a mealy-mouthed compromise at a time in our history which pre-dated the suffragette movement. However, the end of the eighteenth century was not without those handful of women who sought to secure women's rights, and chief among these was one of the earliest feminist philosopher, Mary Wollstonecraft. She died at the young age of 38 and she became better known for her writings long after her death than during her lifetime. It could be said that Orde's relatively feeble attempt to reconcile female education with of male coincided with Wollstonecraft's life, if not entirely with her advocacy for women's right.

Girls should have four Provincial Schools of their own, catering for about eight hundred scholars. This displayed some initiative, at least, and in the light of contemporary thinking on female education such as that

103 Mr Orde's Speech, 57–58.
104 Bolton Manuscripts, Ms. 16,360.

of the church and state in England who 'recognised that a certain proportion of the male population had to be educated in secondary schools and Universities to maintain law and order and to promote the cultural standards of European civilisation … but girls were not included'.[105]

Orde gave some thought to organizing accommodation for girls' education in so far as he said:

> I believe, that there are at present about six hundred girls in the different charter-schools. I would suggest the propriety of providing for the addition of two hundred more, and dispose of them in equal proportions in the four provinces of the kingdom.[106]

Education in the eighteenth century was the preserve of the aristocratic class, and there were distinctly separate curricula laid down for males and females. It was, therefore, unusual for somebody like Thomas Orde to instigate a curriculum for both men and women, with partial overlap.

Likewise, with his thoughts on physical education. He encouraged the notion of physical fitness in the schools for which he had planned. 'Accomplishments of the body were not to be neglected,' he wrote, 'might be made subservient to the purposes of Health and exercise.'[107]

Physical education in schools was not a new idea. In the seventeenth century, John Locke had promulgated the concept of physical training, and this became part of a tri-partite idea including ethics and reasoning. Locke felt that students should be allowed express themselves in different fashions, and just mental agility, but physical agility as well. In his *Some Thoughts Concerning Education,* he included physical development, training the body before the mind would produce a solid temperament to the physical world of the child. Locke also subscribed to the view that both women and men should have access to the same levels of education. Apart from the physical, mental aptitudes of both men and women were equal, he believed.

Orde was concerned with a combination of health and physical activity.[108]

105 N. Hans, *New Trends in Education in the Eighteenth Century,* 194.
106 Mr Orde's Speech, 58.
107 Bolton Manuscripts, Ms. 16,360.
108 J. Giffard, *Mr. Orde's Plan …,* 92.

His debt of gratitude to Hely-Hutchinson did not go amiss when he declared in his speech on 12 April, 1787 that:

> I have particularly to acknowledge obligation to my right honourable friend (the Provost) near me for his assistance upon this, as well as upon many other occasions, in my consideration of this important subject; and I believe myself to be well warranted in bringing forward the declaration of his sentiments, to give weight to my own in this respect, that very great abuses prevail in many of the institutions I have alluded to, by the misapplication of their funds, and the dereliction of their object.[109]

Some evidence emerged in 1785, through the investigations of Jeremiah Fitzpatrick, regarding abuses within the Charter School System, and these reports had a deleterious effect on the Incorporated Society. One such report from the Arklow Charter School insinuated improper relations between the master and the female ushers, and this report resulted in the master's dismissal at the end of the year.[110]

Orde's proposals on education reform, introduced just before his departure from his post as Chief Secretary, had produced a 'potentially dangerous polarisation'.[111] On the one hand, the Anglicans were piqued, while the humanitarians, Holmes, Griffith, Blaquire, and other supporters of prison reform were aligned with Orde and a sense of enlightenment – or, even, irreligion, as Orde's enemies declared.

The 1780s was a decade of extreme activity when a considerable degree of effort and time were devoted to investigations into the circumstances surrounding education in Ireland, followed by the framing of an 'imaginative', if not unrealistic plans for a scheme that would meet the 'needs of all classes', can be viewed as something of a milestone. Though Orde's proposals came to nothing, they did provide the opportunity for educational research and collections of vast amounts of data about schools at the time, and subsequently. It was found that the Charter Schools did not measure

109 Mr Orde's Speech, 91–92.

110 *Freeman's Journal*, 3–6 March 1787.

111 O. MacDonagh, *The Inspector General: Sir Jeremiah Fitzpatrick and Social Reform, 1783–1802* (London: Croom Helm, 1981), 119.

up to the ambitious plans of Hely-Hutchinson and Orde, and this by itself would have marginalized them.[112]

Orde's Plans for Diocesan Schools and Classical Education

In the Chief Secretary's address to parliament in College Green, the classification of tier three was delineated:

> The third should take in the middling ranks of the community, and afford the means, at an easy expence [sic], of a liberal classic education to persons designed for various species of learned professions, and to the gentry of the neighbourhood, who would not choose or could not afford to send their children to schools of a more distant situation and higher expence.[113]

Classical education was not a necessary requirement for entry to the Provincial Schools, but as far as Orde was concerned, it was an essential element of Diocesan education. 'The function of the diocesan schools was to furnish 'gentlemen of small fortune' and aspirants to the professions with a suitable education.[114] He wished for a primal position for classical education within a revamped diocesan school structure. These schools were aimed at the gentry, who would wish to appear among those of their rank of life, with as much advantage as possible in every endowment of the mind and manners.[115] Orde goes some way towards rationalizing the study of a 'dead' language, and, in his speech in the College Green, he devotes considerable content to the pros and cons of such a pedagogical option in the Diocesan Schools and later in University education:

112 See K. Milne, *The Irish Charter Schools 1730–1830* (Dublin: Four Courts Press, 1997), 203.
113 Thomas Orde, *Mr. Orde's Plan of an Improved System of Education in Ireland*, 29.
114 J. Kelly, 'The Context and Course of Thomas Orde's Plan of Education of 1787', 14.
115 J. Giffard, *Mr. Orde's Plan ...*, 61. See also C. McElroy, 'Thomas Orde and Educational Innovation ...', 159.

> Acquiring a language of more general use, but as conducive to the better understanding and improvement of their own. And if we were disposed to penetrate deeply into the antient [sic] derivation or improvement of languages, we should have no great difficulty in tracing a source from which the Grecians themselves drew materials of refinement and perfection in their language, which had at the time the effect of enlarging and improving their general sphere of introduction and knowledge.[116]

Then he speaks in a metaphorical tone when addressing the classics:

> It should be looked upon as a skilful representation of inanimate nature, in the harmonious assemblage and distribution of her most beautiful or romantic scenery, which must form the necessary ground-work for an excellent landscape, but should not go forth from the hand of the artist, as a work of perfection, likely to detain as well as at first to catch the eye of admiration, without a judicious intermixture and variety of living objects and interesting action.[117]

He planned for twenty-two diocesan schools for the whole country. This was a response to the remnants of what was in operation in the 1780s, a situation in which the law on diocesan schools was not being enforced, and some masters were not being paid, while others 'receive the whole of their salary, the better to enable them to reside in idleness at a distance from their schools'.[118] The statute books date back to Tudor legislation in 1570 when Elizabeth I introduced legislation for Diocesan Schools in Ireland. Orde was adamant that these schools should reinstated properly in suitable residences in which accommodation for the scholars would be provided:

> These seminaries [as he calls them], well established, regulated, and overlooked, would afford a very liberal education to many ranks of the community, and speedily work a most favourable change throughout the country. The first step which I conceive it necessary for us to take, in order to carry this object into effect, is to revise the several acts 12 Elizabeth to 29 George 2. For the establishment and maintenance of diocesan schools, and school houses ...[119]

116 Mr Orde's Speech, 97.
117 Mr Orde's Speech, 97–98.
118 J. Giffard, *Mr. Orde's Plan ...*, 65. See C. McElroy, 'Thomas Orde and Educational Innovation ...', 159.
119 Mr Orde's Speech,. 99.

Later, in his speech he alludes to the state of the original Diocesan schools, and we have, 'not only to lament, that the houses are in ruins, and the grounds which have been annexed to them, are now hardly to be retraced, but that too often the master has become an exile, and the disciples are nowhere to be found'.[120] Oddly enough, in the midst of such dilapidation and disarray, the Chief Secretary is hopeful of a full recovery, provided the legislation can be utilized to best advantage.[121]

Perhaps, at this point, it would be timely to digest a segment of Orde's speech in the Commons at College Green:

> Your parish schools, your diocesan schools, but chiefly your schools of richer endowment, have not in general been regarded with the attention they deserved, and which ought to have been paid to them; but there too many examples to be traced of more than neglect; of shameful perversion: There could have been one spirit, and one principle, which, in any view to the public good, might be supposed to have influenced the humane and generous minds of the original founders of these institutions. They must have cherished the natural and the well merited confidence, that ______ 'their bones'
>
> When they had run their course, and slept in blessings,
>
> Should have a tomb of Orphan's tears wept on them.'
>
> But Alas! So has not their memory been revered! The voice of infant gratitude has rarely been instructed to sound the name of their benefactor. It has not often met the eye or reached the ear of the parentless, or of them who had none to teach them. The altars of instruction have been robbed of their incense, too frequently dissipated or consumed by the chosen ministers, who have scarcely designed to chaunt a scanty requiem ...[122]

120 Mr Orde's Speech, 63.

121 Mr Orde's Speech, 63.

122 Thomas Orde-Powlett (Baron Bolton) *Mr. Orde's Plan of an Improved System of Education in Ireland* (Nabu Public Domain Reprints), 23. The full text of Orde's speech in College Green is also available in John Giffard, *Mr. Orde's Plan of an Improved System of Education in Ireland; Submitted to the House of Commons, 12 April 1787; with the Debate Which Arose Thereon* (Dublin: Printed by W. Porter, 1787; Miami: Hard Press, 2019, Reprint), 23.

Orde's interpretation of the diocesan school problem was not with the laws from 1570, but with the failure to implement the legislation. Many of these schools had been neglected over the years, and in some cases, the plot of land attached to them had disappeared. Orde wished that the original appurtenances be reintroduced.

Between 1570 and the late 1700s, several acts of Parliament were instituted regarding the running costs of these schools, but exact amounts were never stipulated. Under the legislation, Anglican bishops were expected to contribute one-third of the total cost with their clergy being responsible for the remainder. The average cost of running one of these schools was about thirty pounds per annum. Orde found that when he had corresponded with the diocesan schoolmasters, many were not able to draw their pay, while others were being paid, though they were without any teaching responsibilities.[123] This situation aroused the ire of Orde, but he had a simple and workable solution: he would increase the bishop's contribution, then he would request that deans and chapters to make a contribution, and a benevolence would be claimed from all persons employed by the bishop. The lay people did not escape, as he intended that all important officers of the county would be asked to contribute, and the following were earmarked – governors, knights, and members of town councils, cities and boroughs. He also felt confident that voluntary contributions would be made towards the running costs of his proposed Diocesan Schools:

> The general property of the counties will, although in a very small degree, be liable to some charge by the necessity of building and maintaining schools and schoolhouses: But I must farther venture to observe, that great officers of the counties within the diocese, such as the governors, the custodes rotulorum, knights of the shire, members for cities, towns or boroughs within the diocese, and certain other persons, might likewise, upon the principle already mentioned, become proper contributors to the fund.[124]

He felt the masters should have reasonably commodious living conditions, with a fixed income, and to ensure they were toeing the line, their schools should have frequent visits from inspectors or other visitors.

123 See C. McElroy, *Thomas Orde, 1746–1807 ...*, 81.
124 Mr Orde's Speech, 67.

In Orde's time there was no set well-defined system of inspection for schools. The earliest school inspection in Ireland is attributed to John Veevers, when he inspected schools under the auspices of the Kildare Place Society in 1818.

Boys attending the Diocesan Schools, under Orde's proposals, would have to pay a modest fee, and if their families could not afford to pay this amount, their schooling was granted *gratis.*[125]

As Orde was concerned with introducing a state-supported national system of education, in which his plan addressed five tiers, it is no wonder that an inspectorate of some sort should play a key role in order to ensure uniformity, constancy and regularity. Unfortunately, systematization taken too far can sometimes lead to tedium, by killing the enthusiasm and *joie de vivre* of an erstwhile exceptionally effective teacher. A system's approach can sometimes be the bedrock upon which fervour, eagerness, keenness and above all, passion, can falter.

Though he was keen to establish such a system in Ireland, and he used his high office as a launching pad from which he unfurled his prototype in April 1787, he never wished to become too involved in the minutiae of teaching, for example. In his speech, or elsewhere, he never dealt with methodology in any detail, or questioning techniques or opening a lesson or closing one, and so forth. He did, however, mention one aspect of methodology, which was in operation in some of the public schools in England, and this involved the students or scholars questioning each other on the topic of the day:

> Nothing will more conduce thereto, than to allow the boys to question and examine each other, under the direction and arbitration of their master. The means of information in other collateral branches of education, such as writing and arithmetic, will of course be provided and attendance enforced; nor should opportunities or encouragement be wanting to improve the accomplishments of the body, as well as

125 Depending on the state of funding, Orde felt a fixed salary might also be paid to one or perhaps two assistants. A small gratuity should also be made available for a writing master, in the hope of obtaining a well-qualified one. He believed a ceiling of £150 should be placed on the combined salaries of staff. See C. McElroy, *Thomas Orde, 1746–1807*, 82n.

> those of the mind, and indeed they may be made subservient to the essential purposes of health and activity, and of emulation and spirit.[126]

Realizing that political support for a system of education was always required, along with ecclesiastical agreement on the finer points, Orde concentrated his efforts on gaining the trust of the Irish House of Commons, in the first place, and in the second place the question of religious animosity did not arise, as his education plan for Ireland *de facto* excluded all but members of the Established Church. In his speech in College Green Orde[127] clearly stated that the 'children should be indispensably brought up in the established religion', Perhaps, there was one encroachment by Orde onto the field of methodology, and that was his attempted modelling of practices in English Grammar Schools where the boys question each other under the guidance of the master. He favoured classroom emulation and inhouse competition among the students, and with scholarships, prizes and exhibitions at the finishing pole, these incentives worked, at least for a while.

He had in mind three scholars per year per province, and their bursary would amount to £25 each year for seven. To fund this, he was hoping for an annual parliamentary grant of £200.

Orde and Collegiate Schools

In his speech, Orde presented his ideas for the fourth tier of education in Ireland, namely, Collegiate Schools. Originally, a proposal put forward by the Provost of the University of Dublin, Trinity College, John Hely-Hutchinson. Orde wished these schools:

> to supply the richest resource of the most polished erudition to the youth of high rank and noblest ambition, whose object and fair pretentions it may be to attempt

126 Mr Orde's Speech, 72.
127 Mr Orde's Speech, 47.

> the first lines of professional distinction, and the highest offices and employments of the state.[128]

Much of Orde's thoughts and plans owe a debt of gratitude to Hely-Hutchinson, and is to be seen in his Outlines of a plan for a great school connected with the University, and some thoughts on school education in Ireland.[129]

What Orde has in mind here is one or two preparatory schools for the university, schools of an elitest nature for boys of genius to prepare them for their future roles in Irish Society. This notion smacks of Plato's idea where political leaders should be highly educated so that as political leaders they would be known as philosopher-kings. Funding would come from:

> that part of the revenue of lands given to the state for the endowment of schools [land that had largely fallen into private hands] be reclaimed and applied consonant with the donor's intentions. In order to provide an educational ladder for boys of genius to climb, exhibitions and other incitements to merit were to be created throughout the system, and especially at the two highest academies.[130]

Initially, he had planned to have a principal in these schools who would manage all the internal economic matters, along the lines of Charterhouse in London, but following reconsideration, and having listened to advice on the matter, he changed his mind, dismissing the idea because such a person would create an additional expense.[131]

Though Orde was flamboyant in his lavish and expansionist ideas for a new system of education for Ireland, there were occasions, as we have seen when his circumspection won the day.

While he not have any deep insight into the most effective methods that could be employed by the teachers in his proposed plans, he was quite willing to accept teachers from schools in England. These would be experienced instructors from some of the great schools such as Eton, Westminster,

128 Mr Orde's Speech, 29.es Speech, 29.e.

129 See Chapter 2 for the 'Outlines'.

130 D. H. Akenson, *The Irish Education Experiment,* 65.

131 J. Giffard, *Mr. Orde's Plan …,* 83.

Harrow, Winchester, and so forth, and bring with them the 'most approved methods of study practised in those seminaries …'[132]

A Second University

In the eighteenth century there was only one university in Ireland, the University of Dublin, with one constituent college, Trinity College. This university came into being in 1595 as a result of Tudor legislation during the reign of Elizabeth 1. It was established as a bastion of Protestantism in Ireland.

In Orde's speech in the House of Commons, not far from Trinity College, he proposed the establishment of a second university. When attempting to introduce such a measure he was mindful of Hely-Hutchinson's response as Provost of TCD. Perhaps, the Provost might view the proposal as a threat to his own institution or even to himself in the role of Provost. One of the locations Orde had in mind was in the northern half of the country:

> I must now take notice of a doubt that is started in respect to the propriety or advantage of sending this additional succession of students to the University of Dublin, wherein the numbers are already much greater than can confessedly, under the present regulations, be sufficiently attended to. Many additional circumstances of very great weight, and which may have important consequences, are adduced as arguments in favour of a new college or university to be established in some central part of the kingdom, to which, perhaps, the school of Armagh should be the immediate nursery of succession, whilst lesser sources of supply might be derived from Enniskillen, Cavan, Raphoe, and other present institutions.[133]

Perhaps, in order to placate Hely-Hutchinson, Orde goes on to find the University of Dublin to be in very sound health and good fettle:

132 Mr Orde's Speech, 84.
133 Mr Orde's Speech, 100.

> It will not be imagined that any idea of injury or discredit to the University of Dublin can have originated this proposition. I am glad, on the contrary, to take this opportunity of declaring my conviction that her celebrity is a just consequence of her intrinsic excellence, and that in effect it must be very difficult to contrive of superior means in most branches of science, for the compleat [sic] education of young men who will seek to avail themselves of such opportunities, than those which are exemplified in Trinity College.[134]

It is clear from the above statement that Orde felt very contented with the status of Trinity College, and he went so far as to suggest that it could act as a model for the second university. However, in his private Notes, he was intent on closing down the University of Dublin and using the buildings as law courts. He wrote, 'of removing the University out of town – and turning the buildings to Courts of Laws. If University removed out of town[sic] – no necessity of a second'.[135]

These sentiments were not included in his House of Common's address. Realizing that a proposal like this could not be rushed, he, more or less had designs on a six-year time frame for the establishment of a second university. At this particular juncture he had no accurate or precise indications as to how a second university might be funded, but very possibly, 'it would be an unqualified charge upon the public'.[136] Neither did he have any precise idea as to the new institution's constitution, or where precisely it might be established. Whatever about the precise details of the 'second' university, Shelburne warmly endorsed Orde's proposal for tertiary expansion in Ireland.[137] Shelburne and Orde were politically close, and the latter had acted as secretary to the former in the Treasury. Orde was 'Shelburne's man', and the *Dublin Morning Post*[138] asserted that Shelburne was 'constantly consulted on the affairs of Ireland', while the *Belfast Newsletter* was convinced that Shelburne's planned return to this kingdom 'is to act as a

134 Mr Orde's Speech, 100–101.

135 J. Giffard, *Mr. Orde's Plan …,* 10. See Colm McElroy, *Thomas Orde, 1746–1807,* 85.

136 J. Giffard, *Mr. Orde's Plan …,* 105.

137 Referenced in N. Aston and C. Campbell Orr, eds, *An Enlightenment Statesman in Whig Britain: Lord Shelburne in Context, 1737–1805* (Woodbridge: Boydell Press, 2011), 86.

138 *Dublin Morning Post,* 23 October 1784.

coadjutor to the Duke of Rutland and Mr. Orde'.[139] Shelburne also backed the Free Trade agreement between the two kingdoms, and this, possibly, had an influence over Orde, 'who was piloting it through the Dublin parliament'.[140] And, in contrast to Pitt, Shelburne did not favour placing the onus on Ireland to contribute financially to the needs of the empire.[141]

In a general comment on education, towards the end of his speech, Orde confirms his die-hard devotion to the union between Great Britain and Ireland, and because of the reciprocal nature of the type of education he had in mind for Ireland, there should exist a free-flowing educational intercourse between the two jurisdictions:

> The reciprocities of this happiest kind of intercourse and connection may therefore grow and multiply upon the successful advancement of this system, and may tend thereby to draw the two countries still closer to each other by a bond of most interesting, yet most disinterested attraction, in assimilating their manners and their suspicions, conciliating their prejudices and suspicions, and concentrating their ambition and affections.[142]

Clearly, the Chief Secretary was a political creature who was bent on creating a culture in Ireland which would enable the country to become more amenable to unification with Great Britain. He was speaking a mere thirteen years before the Acts of Union were passed. These were parallel acts passed in both the Irish House of Commons in College Green and in the British House of Commons at Westminster, in 1800, and received the royal assent on 1 August 1800. This legislation came into force on 1 January 1801, and the merged parliament met for the first time at Westminster on 22 August, 1801.

By the time we encounter Orde on 12 April 1787 his plans are not yet finalized. For instance, he is by this time thinking of one or two collegiate schools, and if there are two, the second one will be attached to the second university. For this university to get off the ground, he had envisaged a

139 *Belfast Newsletter*, 20–24 August 1784.
140 See Aston and Campbell Orr, 152.
141 Aston and Campbell Orr, 152.
142 Mr. Orde's Speech, 103.

Provost, a Vice-Provost, a number of Fellows, perhaps eight or nine, and with that in mind it should mirror the likes of Cambridge or Oxford.

College of Visitors

His next venture, having recognized the complexity of his intentions over a very wide spectrum of reform and rejuvenation, was to adopt a monitoring policy, through the good offices of an inspectorate. Beginning with a modest proposal, he expressed the view that:

> I have now only to return to the more humble idea, with which I began the introduction to this division of the plan, and to submit to your consideration the propriety of countenancing the appointment of three or four learned men, would should assist in the immediate formation of plans and regulations for the several establishments of improved education, and should be invested with a most honourable trust, as the regular inspectors and examiners of them.[143]

Following on from his initial foray into monitoring and inspection he held the concept of a College of Visitors in mind. This would be populated by persons with 'superior qualifications' and whose purpose was to have a duty to constant inspection and examination of the various schools in a revamped Irish education system. More immediately, these persons would have responsibility for drawing up plans and designing regulations around the different sections of the system. This college would be part of the new university, or, perhaps attached to one of the two collegiate schools. In fact, Orde vacillated on the exact location of the College of Visitors. He also thought it would be a good idea to have this institution in Athlone, the exact centre of Ireland. In any case:

> The members should be all fellows, and not confined to the profession of the church, but chosen for their superior knowledge and learning not only in classical studies but in every species of literature and science. They should have a proper annual income

143 Mr Orde's Speech, 118.

> ...., proper Apartments-Hall-Chapel, etc., and a regular economical provision for their common table. Their number might in the end be 7, 8, or 9 with a Principal.[144]

It was envisaged that these inspectors would make a 'circuit' of the country visiting various institutions which were under the auspicious of the government. As well undertaking supervision of classroom practice, including teaching effectiveness, organization and discipline, they were also encouraged to carry out an audit of the schools' accounts. Particular attention had to be paid to students who were potential candidates for exhibitions or studentships at either of the two universities. If required the inspectors could 'borrow' staff members from either of the universities to assist them in examining the boys.

Initially, Orde strongly believed that these inspectors should be Englishmen, and especially 'men who are or have been engaged either in the universities or in some of the great schools in teaching the several branches of literature and science'.[145] Inducements would be associated with this proposal – proper accommodation, pensions and preferments would be on offer after a given time. Their lifestyles should be made as comfortable as possible, where convenience, 'health and prosecution of studies in the buildings and grounds to be attached to them'.[146]

In attracting persons of eminence from these well-established English institutions, Orde hoped that they might commit their reports to paper and hopefully have their reflections published.

The Chief Secretary was perennially concerned about costings, and his plan for Irish education was no exception. However, with so few inspectors associated with his plans, he felt that the expenses might not be too onerous on the kingdom, and the country might, in fact, be compensated by the increased contribution the College of Visitors would make to Ireland.

James Kelly offers a terse and pithy summary of Thomas Orde's plans for Irish education:

144 Bolton Manuscripts, Ms. 16,372, 2–3. This number of inspectors, in an age of the horse and carriage, seems very inadequate with such a vast array of institutions to manage.

145 J. Giffard, *Mr. Orde's Plan ...*, 11.

146 J. Giffard, *Mr. Orde's Plan ...*, 12.

> Orde's plan of education was the most sophisticated and ambitious proposal for educational reform yet proposed in Ireland. In effect, it was an attempt to reconstitute that part of the existing system represented by the Parish and Diocesan schools; to integrate those parts represented by the Royal, Charter, and Erasmus Smith schools into the Parish and Provincial schools; to introduce new branches of education in the form of the Provincial and Collegiate schools, and to double the university sector.[147]

Reflection and Conclusion

In Thomas Orde's speech in the Irish House of Commons on 12 April 1787, we find the following comment – 'I hope that some liberal and extensive plan for the general improvement of education will be matured for an early execution.'[148] Orde, of course, was ideally placed in order to advance the administration's commitment to the conservative Protestant position. Indeed, the Chief Secretary had little time for Catholic demands on the grounds that 'measures which ... tended to establish with more firmness and security the ascendancy of Protestants'[149] were more necessary.

The Enlightenment came to dominate European thought during the eighteenth century and with this education came under the focus of various reforms and modernization. The social order could be reconstructed according to scientific principles. Human reason could cure humankind of all its ills – social, political, economic – leading to peace and utopia.

Following the two revolutions (American and French) the re-education of the people would be scientifically, rationally and progressively underpinned. Faith in rationality was the cornerstone of this movement.

147 James Kelly, 'The Context and Course of Thomas Orde's Plan of Education of 1787', 15.

148 Thomas Orde, *Mr. Orde's Plan for an Improved System of Education in Ireland, Submitted to the House of Commons, 12 April 1787; with the Debate That Arose Thereon* (Dublin, 1787), 3.

149 Gerard O' Brien, ed., *Parliament, Politics and People: Essays in Eighteenth-Century Irish History* (Dublin: Irish Academic Press, 1989), 121.

Obliterating poverty, hunger, superstition, persecution and war was the ultimate aim, which would have serious implications for education. Education would have to adopt its strategies in areas like methodology, and it would have a new role in sociological terms. If people were innately good, then the future would have the unspoiled child, an uncorrupted and natural being whose interests, needs and inclinations were the proper beginnings of instruction. Education was to be an instrument for social reform. This is the milieu in which Thomas Orde operated, and he was not found wanting when the time came for him to act.

The Enlightenment threw up the likes of Montesquieu, Voltaire, Diderot and Rousseau. Let's concern ourselves briefly with Rousseau. He believed that human beings are naturally good, with an inborn love of themselves and a compassion for others. They are happy, nature provides for them, and does not fill them with tempting and corrupting illusions; they are free, equal and happy. But, society corrupts this state of nature (the Noble Savage) by creating the laws of property and by creating unnatural desires. Particularly pernicious is the development of desires which the individual cannot fulfil, and this develops 'amour-propre' (pride, love of flaunting oneself).

In short, to counteract the foregoing frailties children must be taught never to desire what they themselves cannot provide in their immediate environment. In other words, they must be protected from seductive illusions in society. And, to achieve this, they must be kept active and constantly exercising.

Rousseauistic principles were advanced by Pestalozzi and Froebel at a later stage, and their effects were felt in Ireland during the next century, especially towards the end. However, by the end of the eighteenth-century educational reform was firmly on the agenda of the state.

In the meantime, Orde had been criticizing education in Ireland by stating that 'nothing can be more fruitless or preposterous than the arrangement at present', and asserted that 'the interference of government is therefore necessary'.[150]

150 Orde's Speech in the House of Commons, 25.

He displayed a genuine concern for the plight of the Irish people, and he felt that an inspiring education system would enable the populace to drag themselves out of the mire in which they found themselves. His plan was thorough, it was extensive – more than any other attempt, but, and he admitted that 'Catholics will not send their children to Protestant English schools'. Why, if he realized this, did he insist that the teachers in his plan must be Protestant? In one fell swoop, he denied success to his own plan, which, if implemented, would have been of great benefit to Ireland, and it would have pre-dated the national system of the 1830s by a half-century.

Orde's proposals involved a complete restructuring of education in Ireland with a five-tier system designed to cover all peoples and classes in Irish society. His plan represented the start of the changing mentality of the state and the use of education within a new government rationale. It was the first time that a mixed (multi-denominational) system, with children of all denominations taught in the same classroom, was promulgated as a governmental policy aimed at the welfare of the whole Irish population. It was proposed to appoint four men to formulate the plans and regulations for the various institutions, also acting as inspectors and examiners of the institutions. This represents a shift in policy, with a pseudo-centralized administration to maintain the system, thus giving the state control over institutions that were previously controlled by the Christian denominations in Ireland. This was, without doubt, a new departure. Thomas Orde acknowledged his plan as being ambitious, and stated that as no system of this magnitude existed elsewhere, the creation of the tiered education system was to act as 'model to the world'.[151] He was also cautious enough to thread carefully:

> It will not be conceived that I have formed the romantic expectation of being able to execute at once every division of so extensive a scheme. We may take a sample of each, except that I do not venture to hope, we may go farther for the people.[152]

The Chief Secretary's efforts in proposing a widespread and all-encompassing plan for Irish education came to nought. Government,

151 J. Giffard, *Mr. Orde's Plan …*, 11.
152 J. Giffard, *Mr. Orde's Plan …*, 11.

subsequent governments took up the mantle and carried out several worthwhile and crucial researches into Irish education, both from the standpoint of provision, but also the efficacy of execution.

By the time Orde arrived in Ireland, the inadequacy of the different levels of education was blatantly obvious. There had existed for many decades a certain lethargy or ennui with regard to energizing education in Ireland. The finances were there, for the most part, but they were badly managed, or, worse, they were being misdirected.

Orde was alert to these issues, and that allied to his own investigations into the matter, signalled in him a feeling that something urgent was required. He took it upon himself to design a procedure that would address these issues, not immediately, but in a piecemeal adaptation, which would not be bereft of the necessary gravity of the matter in hand. Diversity was one of the key principles within his framework, as without it full accommodation of the assorted denominations in Ireland would not be accomplished.

Without extolling Orde's virtuosity beyond credibility, it is necessary, all the same, to ascribe a certain degree of an encapsulating viewpoint on his behalf when it comes a system of education. Notwithstanding the *de facto* omission of two portions of the population, Catholics and Presbyterians, with a combined percentage of between 80 and 90, it defies credulity that Orde believed his plan would work without the cooperation of these two denominations. Hindsight can wield an accurate axe, but, even in the heat of the moment the Chief Secretary must have garnered some semblance of attitudinal matter from one or other of the groupings. If he had not accumulated any worthwhile insight into his preparations prior to April 12, then the word candour springs to mind. His planned system of education placed a certain degree of emphasis on the local community's contribution and involvement, mainly through the local clergyman, the magistrate, along with the community providing the teacher's residence.

Be that as it may, and with Orde's undoubted determination, his plan may have worked, provided concessions were made to the church bodies, including the Church of Ireland, as they did not wish to be burdened by such an onerous ordeal. Hely-Hutchinson suggested to Orde that it would be advantageous to have an inventory of the endowed and state-sponsored schools in Ireland. At the close of 1785, the Chief Secretary wrote in the margins of proposals for a scheme of education sent to him by the Provost, Hely-Hutchinson, who had suggested the Charter Schools should be investigated, Orde was also concerned about the Royal and Diocesan schools. As early as April 1786 the Chief Secretary requested that the Irish House of Commons in College Green should order that returns be acquired about the schools in question and detailing their various types and their pedagogical aspirations. Orde was eager to have this done, and he had preempted what the Provost had in mind, and had already begun the process of investigation. During 1786, he had made contact with various members of the Anglican Hierarchy to establish the number and status of schools which were operating under the auspices of the Crown.[153]

Early, in his speech in the House of Commons, College Green, Orde implored his listeners to help deal with the situation in which Irish education was currently situated. He said:

> In many cases (and I trust it may be so in this) the universality and excess of a malady excite a more general exertion of consideration and skill, and give thereby a greater chance of remedy and cure. Nothing is wanting here but the simple effort to overcome indifference or despondency. Cease to vent your feelings in this respect, as you are now heard to do, by fruitless lamentations or idle reproaches on the defects of your present system, or rather upon the want of any system at all. Give the animation which is due to your sensibility, and do not hesitate at the attempt to become an example of more general perfection than has been seen in any country.[154]

Orde, in his short three years as Chief Secretary, was one the first to realize that Ireland needed more than a collection of different types of schools: Ireland needed a comprehensive education system.[155] He undertook an investigation into the existing schools in 1786, and he found the 'damp of neglect has struck upon them, and they are mildewed'. He had found 'shameful' neglect, and he expressed the wish to extend education to all parts of the community. He found much worse than 'neglect' as he also uncovered what he called 'shameful perversion'. In his plan we can detect a strong element of upward mobility thinking. Thus, the idea of a

153 See Bolton Manuscripts, Ms. 15887 (1).

154 Mr Orde's Speech, 10.

155 D. H. Akenson, *The Irish Education Experiment ...*, 68.

system for Irish education was put forward very forcibly in his speech in the Irish House of Commons on 12 April 1787:

> The Right Hon. Mr. Orde moved, that that part of the Lord Lieutenant speech, at the opening of the present session, which respects public education, be now read; it was read accordingly in the following words:
>
> I hope that some liberal and extensive plan for the general improvement of education will be matured for an early execution.
>
> Mr. Orde then moved, that the House do forthwith resolve itself into a committee of the whole House, to take the foregoing paragraph into consideration.
>
> The House resolved itself into a committee accordingly, Mr. Solicitor General in the chair.[156]

There is a strong hint in the early part of his speech in the Irish House of Commons that the Chief Secretary had a genuine desire to improve the circumstances of the Irish people. One of the avenues through which this could take place was by offering the youth of Ireland 'an opportunity of bringing out and improving talents, with which nature may have endowed him, fitted to a rank superior to that which nature had allotted him'.[157]

One of his proposals centred about the replacement of Henry VIII's statute of 1537 with a new scheme for a systematic approach to educational provision in Ireland. His plan envisaged the erection of schools in every parish supported by a fund raised from the taxation of the Anglican clergy and its benefices and the more opulent landlords. The funds for the Erasmus

156 *Mr. Orde's Plan of an Improved System of Education in Ireland* (Dublin: House of Commons, 12 April 1787; Nabu Public Domain Reprints, n.d.), 3. See also, John Giffard, *Mr. Orde's Plan of an Improved System of Education in Ireland; Submitted to the House of Commons, 12 April 1787; with the Debate Which Arose Thereon* (Dublin: Printed, W. Porter, Skinner-Row, 1787), 3. This has been reprinted by HardPress Classics, Miami, 2019.

157 T. Orde, 'A System of Education' (Oxford: Bodleian Library, Ms. Top Irel, d. 2), 5. Quoted in Norman Atkinson, *Irish Education: A History of Educational Institutions* (Dublin: Allen Figgis, 1969), 65.

Smith Schools and the Charter Schools[158] would be re-directed towards the new schools, including four provincial colleges.

By the time we get to April 1787, we find that any romantic or picturesque notions entering his plans for Irish education have been duly knocked sideways. In his speech on April 12 he states unequivocally that:

> I am not about to propose to you any visionary or romantic plans. You shall see them all capable of execution. The first object which must naturally engage the attention, in bringing the business forward to this state, is that of expence [sic].[159]

And, on the question of expense, he continues in a very rational and plain-speaking manner:

> .... I shall not of course be so far misconceived, as to have any opinion entertained of my being able to provide the means of support and success, for a variety of new or enlarged establishments, without any call upon you for additional aid and protection; but I will venture to persuade myself of your assent to this proposition, that the charge I shall after all be obliged to suggest for the public incumbrance, will fall much below an adequate proportion to the benefits which it is intended to purchase.[160]

Orde's education plan was in itself one of great scope and detail, 'worthy of Pitt himself'.[161] From the bottom up, there were to be parish schools, four provincial schools to displace the charter schools, grammar-school-type curriculum in the Diocesan Schools, and two well-endowed 'great schools' in which youths of distinction would receive a first class classical[162] education.

158 The schools of the Incorporated Society, generally called 'charter schools' after the Society's royal mandate, were seen as agents of that very improvement so much sought after by the pamphlet writers. Indeed their hopes for Ireland's economic future were bound up with a Whig view of how society was to be ordered, and the free constitution of that order had no place for popery. See Kenneth Milne, 'Irish Charter Schools', *The Irish Journal of Education*', *8/1* (1974), 3–29.

159 Mr Orde's Speech, 20.

160 Mr Orde's Speech, 21.

161 R. B. McDowell, *Ireland in the Age of Imperialism and Revolution, 1760–1801* (Oxford: Clarendon Press, 1979), 93–94.

162 A classical education was the mark of a gentleman. John Locke had urged that Latin and Greek should be taught only to gentlemen: those intended for careers in commerce should learn subjects pertaining to directly to the future lives. See

Though Orde welcomed children from all walks of life and from all denominations, he did stipulate that children who were maintained at the state's expense should be brought up in the religion of the state, the established religion. Orde was very conscious of the value of bursaries, exhibitions, distinctions and scholarships, and expected 'boys of genius' to raise themselves from the lowest to the highest rank. A medical professor, Stephen Dickson, from Trinity College was very critical of this aspect of Orde's proposals. He claimed it would produce a 'swarm' of indignant, unemployed scholars. It was a mistake, Dickson argued, 'to increase the competition in any employment disproportionately to the profits arising from the exercise of that employment'.[163] One other critic, William Drennan[164] assaulted Orde's scheme of 'education by statute' for its inflexibility and for placing education under the wing of the Anglican Church and state. 'Establishments,' he said, 'are always decaying. Individuals are always in a state of progressive amelioration.'[165] Instead, he wished the state should 'assist the manufacture of the mind' by grants to individuals or private institutions engaged in educational enterprise. 'Encourage, but not endow', he wrote.

Orde was very keen to ease his listeners in the Irish House of Commons into a relaxed but supportive spell for his wish to be undertaken with the appropriate amount of zeal and ardour. He was fully aware that if his proposals were not accepted by the members in College Green, his efforts could have come to nought. He was also very aware that his plan was a unique one, and because of that, it should be emulated elsewhere in the world: He urged:

> Give then the model to the world, and be yourselves the first instances of its practicability, and superior excellence. You are capable of its adoption, and you will deserve the triumph of its accomplishment. Look then to your fellow subjects of all ranks with zeal and interest for their improvement, but cast your earliest, your most benign and considerate regard

---

Crowley, T. *Language and History: Theories and Texts* (London: Routledge, 1996). A classical education was seen as the gateway to a proper understanding of the English language.

163 See *Parliamentary Register, Ireland*, vii, 486–505.

164 William Drennan, 1754–1820, physician, patriot, poet. Drennan was a Belfast Presbyterian who hoped for Irish parliamentary reform. He became involved in radical politics with Wolfe Tone and Robert Emmet.

165 *Parliamentary Register, Ireland*, vii, 486–505.

upon the lowest orders of the people. They are after all most necessary to you as the great ground-plot of the scene, upon whose bosom all your beauties are to rise, and which is to be intermixed and harmonized with every part of your prospect.[166]

He was also very earnest in ensuring that the members of the House were fully aware that his plan was not just pie in the sky, and that it was preceded by an accumulation of knowledge about the contemporary state of education in Ireland. To this end, he stated:

It would indeed, be unpardonable in me to have appeared before you upon a subject, and with propositions of the kind, which I have to submit to you, if I had not studied to foresee and to call for and to provoke the objections and obstacles which might be offered or obtruded against so extraordinary a measure. I have, of course, sought to remove such as appeared to be within the compass of my ability, and I humbly indulge a hope that I am prepared to point out to you, how You may dissipate or subdue the rest.[167]

Orde received general support from the members of parliament in Dublin, but there was an unfavourable retort from one M. P., Arthur Browne, representing Trinity College, complained that the university had not been consulted, but this remained a minor issue, as Hely-Hutchinson, the Provost, was ageing and there was nobody else to take up the mantle on behalf of the University of Dublin, or, indeed for that matter, on behalf of education in Ireland. That the education debate in Ireland died prematurely with the departure of Orde in 1787 is a reflection of the malaise with which Orde's efforts were met with in parliament in April 1787.[168]

166 Mr Orde's Speech, 11.
167 Mr Orde's Speech, 12–13.
168 Orde, the Chief Secretary did not confine his attentions solely to an education bill. He, as we have seen, became involved with a commercial trade agreement between Ireland and Great Britain. His Dublin Police Bill of 1786 provoked certain controversy, with strong parliamentary opposition and a fervent public alarm. This was a proposal to establish a police force under the control of Dublin Castle, but it aroused old anxieties about standing armies and ushered in woeful warnings about the decay Dublin's constitution which a continuing accumulation of power by the government would bring about. See S. H. Palmer, *Police and Protest in England and Ireland, 1780–1850* (Cambridge: Cambridge University Press, 1988), 71–73, 92–104.

CHAPTER 4

Orde's Legacy and Reactions to His Plan

Introduction

Orde's plan for Irish education had much to contend with as there were varying vested interest groups and individuals who held very strong ideas about a certain course of education for Ireland. Would Orde receive enough backing for his plan, so that it would reach the reading stage in the Irish House of Commons and find itself on the stepping stone to an Act of Parliament? This chapter addresses Fitzherbert's role in promoting commissioners' reports, in particular that of 1791 and its principal findings; the chapter also deals with the reaction of the press to Orde's education plan; the Churches' response is put forward, namely, the Catholic, Presbyterian and Anglican denominations; Parliamentary responses to the plan are highlighted, as is a response from Edward Tighe (Melantius). The chapter ends with a general comment and conclusion.

Following Orde's departure from Ireland in 1787, the appointment of Alleyne Fitzherbert[1] as Chief Secretary did not mean an end to educational

1 In a long letter of seven pages the Prime Minster, William Pitt the Younger, wrote to the Duke of Rutland, the Lord Lieutenant of Ireland, in October 1785 informing him that Fitzherbert would not under any circumstances replace Orde as Chief Secretary. Pitt had three other possible options in mind in 1785; the first was William Wyndham Grenville, who in 1790 was created Baron Grenville, but Pitt was not sure he would accept the offer; the second was Thomas Steele, for many years Secretary to the Treasury (coincidentally, so was Orde immediately before his appointment as Chief Secretary), and Steele sounded very agreeable to Pitt; the third person was Mr Faulkner, whom Pitt rated very highly, as he was clever

activity. The seeds for research and planning in education were sown by Orde, and this approach was to continue from his time and throughout the next century. Fitzherbert was the first government official to establish a commission to investigate the business of education, and this commission began its work in 1788 and reported in 1791.[2]

In March 1788 Fitzherbert, who had moved for a commission to be established to inquire into the funds and revenues, both public and private, given for the endowment of schools. It was further to inquire into the condition of such schools, and to make recommendations for the improvement of education for the youth of Ireland. In the setting up of this commission recognition was given to the importance of elementary education within society, and to the rights of all individuals to avail of education. Fitzherbert had a solid interest in education, though his bill had a precarious existence, and it came to nothing. The details seem to have disappeared into the ether.[3]

The 1791 Report was all-embracing, from parish schools, with teachers' residences, to the existing charter schools which will receive 'great encouragement and great improvements', to diocesan schools which will be rendered much more useful by the establishment of an additional master, and will receive a classical education along with subjects such as mathematics, to the Royal Schools, all seven of them to be rendered more efficient, to a Collegiate School, or school connected to the University, to a new type of school, the Professional Academy, for those entering the navy, the army

and proved himself as such while working on the Privy Council. Is it possible that any or none of these three potential candidates were available in the year 1787, the actual year in which Orde was departing the scene? No copy of Rutland's reply to Pitt has survived among the papers, but from Pitt's next letter to the Duke there is no doubt that Orde has been completely exonerated by Pitt. See John Duke, *Correspondence between the Right Honble; William Pitt and Charles Duke of Rutland, Lord Lieutenant of Ireland, 1781–1787* (London: William Blackwood and Sons, 1890), 125–132. For Orde's exoneration, see Pitt to Rutland, Holwood Hill, 13 Nov. 1785, in *Correspondence between the Right Honble,* 132–133.

2 This report was not published until the mid-1850s. *Report of Her Majesty's Commissioners appointed to enquire into the endowments, funds and actual condition of all schools endowed for the purpose of education in Ireland,* H.C. 1857-8 (2336-111).

3 See D. H. Akenson, *The Irish Education Experiment,* 70, note 30.

and the commercial world, and one of these is expected to be established in the principal towns of Ireland.

The 1791 *Report of the Commissioners*

The Chief Secretary's efforts in the realm of education may not have sparkled enough during Orde's time in Ireland, but a train of events was set in motion that eventually led to a national system of education in 1831, *albeit* without any legislation, and not nearly as comprehensive as Orde's grand plan. The plan was presented to a conservative parliament, both 'attitudinally and fiscally' and Orde was prepared to proceed gradually, but his early departure 'meant his energy was replaced by circumspection and his commitment by caution, with the result that Orde's plan of education became a monument to effort rather than achievement'.[4] However, though not disregarding Kelly's final sentence, a year later the Irish parliament passed a bill to establish a commission of inquiry into the state of Irish education, and it reported in 1791.[5] This report followed on from the work of Orde, surveying the existing situation with regard to education provision in Ireland; parish schools; diocesan schools; royal free schools; Erasmus Smith schools; charter schools, King's Hospital school; and a few others, such as the Hibernian School for Soldiers' children and the Hibernian Marine school, both of which were publicly-funded charity schools. The 1791 Report made radical recommendations; parish

4 James Kelly, 'The Context and Course of Thomas Orde's Plan of Education of 1787', 24.

5 *Commons Jn. Ire.*, xii, pt. i, 402, 411, 419; *Ir. Parl. Reg.*, vii (18 April 1788). An Act to enable the lord lieutenant, or other chief governor or governors of kingdom, to appoint commissioners for enquiring into the several funds and revenues granted by public or private donations for the purposes of education in this kingdom, 28 Geo.III, c. 15[Ire], 1788. See Susan Parkes, *A Guide to Sources for the History of Irish Education, 1780–1922* (Dublin: Four Courts Press, 2010), 26–28. The 1791 Commissioners' Report was not published until 1858. See D. H. Akenson, *The Irish Education Experiment*, 59–69, 70.

schools should be run by a board of governors, with mixed denominations, breaking the monopoly of the Anglican Church; diocesan school numbers to increase to one per county; a new collegiate 'great' school, with classical education, to prepare students for university; an academy also to teach science, mathematics and modern languages. The report was seriously critical of the Charter Schools which, it stated, were in need of complete reform. Among the evils of Charter Schools were 'the ignorance, gross neglect, and fraud of the masters and mistresses'; the children were worked too hard, the allowance for their upkeep was inadequate; sufficient attention wasn't paid to their health.[6] The commissioners of 1791 recommended that the number of Charter Schools be reduced and that their nurseries be abolished. They anticipated a decline in the demand for Charter Schools with the introduction of the scheme for Parish Schools which their report was to propose.[7]

The most important proposal of the lot was that in future there should be no distinction made between religious denominations. Orde had touched upon this principle, but his version was laid bare to frenzied attack. The Report was a pioneering instrument in addressing governance of schools, curriculum, access and teacher supply. Its format would be duplicated many times during the next century, and it, perhaps, left a paradigm of inquiry to be copied and emulated by many.

The 1791 Report addressed many issues, including the Act of 28 Henry VIII, which had set up the parish schools, but, it was said to be 'defective in making no provision for the education of the poor'.[8] In this report, the Charter Schools were most severely deprecated. It was reported that:

> ... in most of the said establishments the instruction, cleanliness, and health of the children had been most grossly neglected; that they had not been allowed sufficient food, clothing, or other necessaries; that in many of these schools they are half starved, half naked, and covered with cutaneous disorders, the effects of filth and

6 *Report of the Commissioners*, 1791, Appendix I, 17–19.

7 *Report of the Commissioners*, 1791, Appendix I, 17–19.

8 Copy of report of the commissioners of Irish education enquiry (1791), in report of the commissioners appointed to inquire into the endowments, funds and actual conditions of all schools endowed for the purpose of education in Ireland, vol. I, p. 2.

> negligence, while in some of those the children of the masters and mistresses appear fresh, clean and in good health.[9]

In their concluding remarks, the Commissioners observed that none of the schools on public foundation, charter schools, parish schools, royal schools or diocesan schools had answered the intentions of their founders, and that with few exceptions they had been of little use to the public.

Michael Quane, in his 'The Diocesan Schools – 1570–1870', casts a cold eye over these schools as they existed in Orde's time. There is a feeling from the following passage that opposition to the Act of Elizabeth I was apparent *ab initio* as it:

> Indicated that there would be a disinclination by those concerned with the execution and administration of its provisions to exercise their functions spontaneously or zealously. History records that throughout the succeeding three centuries, during which the Act existed, it was only partly effective in most of the Protestant dioceses, it was only sporadically observed, and was generally treated as a 'dead letter'. From the very first, it tended to be the conspicuous failure which the passage of time proved it.[10]

However, it was proposed that with some reorganization these schools could provide the structure for a more comprehensive system of education. The recommendations of the Commissioners related primarily to parochial schools. On a first reading the proposals made seem remarkable for their time. However, when they are seen within the context of developments in the last quarter of the eighteenth century they are not out of place. It was the era of Thomas Orde's elaborate and unprecedented plan for Irish education; it was the era of the great civil rights campaign for Catholics; it was the time of the radical and utilitarian movements, when the right of 'all' to receive education was uppermost in the minds of intellectuals; it was the era of the Enlightenment, which produced thinking along the lines that education could act as a social engineering agent. All these ideas were reflected in the 1791 Report. The belief that education was not the prerogative of the privileged minority was seen in

9 1791 Report, 17.

10 Michael Quane, 'The Diocesan Schools – 1570–1870', *Journal of the Cork Historical and Archaeological Society* (Jan.–June 1961), 31, 26–49.

the criticism levied against the existing parish school system, where provision had not been made for the education of the poor. The right to receive education without religious interference was recognized, and marked a crucial sea-change. The Report stated that '… it is our opinion that the children of Roman Catholics and Protestants should be admitted indiscriminately into the schools …'[11] The system of education put forward was a multi-denominational one. The needs of different children were recognized with regard to religious education, and provision was made for this. The Commissioners stated their opinion:

> … that the clergy of each persuasion should attend for the purpose of instructing the children belonging to their respective communions in the principles of religion.[12]

This was not what Orde had in mind; he favoured all children of varying persuasions attending the same school, but being instructed in religion class on the principles of the Church of Ireland.

The 1791 Report reflected the ideas on civil rights and the radical and utilitarian philosophy emerging at the time, and seen in that context it was not as it were 'radical'. However, the severe criticism levied against the existing system, and in particular the Charter Schools, together with the liberal proposals it put forward may have been the reason for its not receiving publication. It was considered by the Commissioners of 1806–1812, and some of the proposals of the 1791 Commission are to be found in their reports.

The Commissioners of 1789–1791 addressed themselves to the task which subsequent committees were also to face: how to devise a plan of education which would be acceptable to Catholics but which wouldn't endanger the Constitution by making political concessions. At the time the report was being prepared there was little reason to be concerned about a Catholic conspiracy. The report itself refers to the complete lack of any 'disaffection' such as was referred to in in the Charter which was granted to the Incorporated Society.

11 1791 Report, 3.
12 1791 Report, 3.

The *Report* recommended that a proper system of parish Schools be established:

> The children of Roman Catholics and Protestants should be admitted indiscriminately into the schools and that the clergy of each persuasion should attend for the purpose of instructing the children belonging to their respective Communions in the principles of religion.[13]

This would have removed exclusive control of the school from the hands of the parson and would have obliged him to share it with Roman Catholics, when Catholics were still disenfranchised and needed a licence before they themselves could teach.

That separate religious instruction be provided on the school premises was a proposal that was certainly at variance with the philosophy of the existing institutions of education. The Commissioners had criticized in strong terms the principal pillar of Protestant education of the time, the Charter Schools, and it may have been the severity of its criticism of the conventional wisdom which caused the Report not to be published and not to be presented to Parliament.

Clearly, a certain amount of ground was being conceded, by granting the Catholics their nominations to the board of governors and by allowing Catholic religious instruction by the priest in the school building. The Report was not implemented, however, and it is not known how acceptable it might have been to Catholics.

As in the scheme proposed by Orde in 1787, effective control would have rested with the Parochial clergy of the Church of Ireland. Orde spoke of this role as, '... as the peculiar province of the minister of the Parish'.[14] In the recommendation of the 1791 Report, the Parson would have been expected to inspect and visit the school; examine the progress of the children and instruct the members of his own faith in the principles of religion. He would have been bound to these duties by oath, taken before the local

13 *Report of the Commissioners*, 1791, Appendix 1, 3.

14 J. Giffard, *Mr. Orde's Plan of an Improved System of Education in Ireland as Submitted to the House of Commons 12 April 1787*, 41.

magistrate. He would also have been obliged to present an annual report on the school in his parish to the board recommended in the Report.[15]

This would have been in some respects a curtailment of the Parson's responsibilities in education. Under the Statute of 28 Henry VIII, C115 he himself was obliged 'to keep or cause to be kept' a school to learn English. The Report of 1791 recommended that he be freed from this obligation.

However, according to the recommendations of 1791 the Parson would have been expected to take an oath before a civil authority and this would presumably have exposed him to civil sanction if found in default of his civil duty. The 1791 Report extended Orde's thesis, but kept a close eye on denominational issues, which in Ireland were never far from the surface, and if not handled circumspectly could render the whole educational edifice chaotic and unworkable.

The investigation of the Commission had uncovered such an amount of dishonesty, negligence and incompetence among the clergy responsible for providing education in the case of the diocesan and parochial schools and for supervising it in the case of Charter Schools,[16] that it may have been felt that the oath taken by an incumbent upon entering his parish did not provide a sufficient guarantee for clergy unwilling to observe the obligations entered into. It was a portent of things to come in the civil legislation which was resorted to, to improve residency among ministers in the nineteenth century.

While the evidence gathered by the Commission of 1791 raised serious doubts as to the suitability of the Church of Ireland as the supervisory agent in an Irish education system, the recommendations envisaged that it should continue in this role, though the obligation to establish a school would be a civil obligation as well as an ecclesiastical one. Both Catholic and Protestant children would attend school, to be taught by a Protestant master, in a system organized by the Church of Ireland and based on the Church of Ireland benefices.

15 *Report of the Commissioners,* 1791, Appendix 1, 3.

16 A Church of Ireland minister was appointed to visit each school and act as a catechist. He was also expected to make a monthly report to the Committee of fifteen. See Report for 1791, Appendix 1, 17.

One reason for this was that there was nobody else. Absenteeism was high among the clergy but was much higher among landowners of whom a half to a third were regularly absent.[17] As such, the clergy represented a class of 'middling gentry' who, by their presence in the community would contribute to a general heightening of the level of culture.

With the gradual improvement in the living conditions of Catholics, the Inquiry was an opportunity to devise a system of education which would integrate Catholics into the life of the State. Catholics did not appear to present a threat to the State having lived in peace for almost a century. The Inquiry was also a tacit admission of the need to control the new system of education developing among Catholics as the pay schools gained in popularity. This growth was to continue and was itself a sign of a growing self-assurance among Catholics.

From a practical point of view, the Report of 1791 was ill-timed, as the decade proved to be an eventful one with religious and agrarian unrest, in 1798 the United Irishmen were involved in a rising. As a result, educational policy took a back seat. However, subsequent commissioners' reports are replete with the language of the 1791 document, and that paved the way for a system that, perhaps, treated Catholics and Protestants equally. But, then, history can have a habit of being unkind, and the future of this policy is for another day.

Orde saw education as a primal force in raising the poor people of Ireland out of the economic mire to which they were hostages. To that end he saw education as a means of infusing 'the balm of information into the wound of ignorance'. And, also in his speech he attributed 'all the violent and atrocious acts which had too often disgraced this nation … to a want of education'.

It could be claimed that Orde set in motion a train of events that culminated in the establishment of the national board of education in 1831. During those decades many investigations into Irish education were undertaken by officialdom, each one in turn leading closer and closer to what society could accept for the mutual benefit of both Catholic and

17 James A. Froude, *The English in Ireland in the Eighteenth Century*, 2 vols (London: Longmans, Green and Co., 1872), 2: 192.

Protestant persuasions. Perhaps, we should inveigle the succinct and precise description by Joseph Doyle, to clarify some of the intricacies of the period following Orde's pronouncements in the House of Commons in College Green on 12 April 1787:

> The period 1787 to 1830 is generally seen as one of successive official initiatives to put in place a system of primary education acceptable to the principal denominations that would satisfy the demand, on the one hand, from the masses for a functional system of secular education, and, on the other, from the ruling elite for a moral underpinning of the status quo.[18]

It was Orde who instigated the concept of a welcome for all religious persuasions in state-supported schools. This mixed education principle, laudable as it may seem, caused much furore when it was actually introduced in the national system in 1831. Orde believed that children who were maintained (food was available in some of the existing Protestant schools) and educated at state expense should be brought up in the established religion. In effect, the Chief Secretary's attempt at introducing an education Bill in 1787 was a mechanism of binding Catholics and Dissenters to the state, and in *The Prelateiad*[19] this endeavour is written as an enlightenment effort –

> To make the SUN of SCIENCE 'lume our isle,
> Tho' Priestly craft, and IGNORANCE profound,
> And BIGOTRY'S imperious mists surround; -
> Removing PREJUDICE'S noxious root, -
> Engrafting EDUCATION'S lib'ral shoot

18 Joseph Doyle, *Model Schools – Model Teachers? A Nineteenth-Century Irish Teacher-Training Initiative* (Kilkenny: Geata Buidhe Books, 2020), 17.

19 *Prelateiad; or the Rape of the Holy Bottle, a heroi-tragi-comic poem*. Written in the time of spiritual wars, 1788/9? Printed by H. Chamberline, College Green, Dublin 2. See T. O'Sullivan, 'Between Toleration and Preservation: The Popery Laws and Irish Anglicanism, 1782–1808', *New Perspectives on the Penal Laws* (Dublin: Eighteenth-Century Ireland, Special Issue, no. 1, 2011), 260–261. The *Prelateiad* was written under the banner of 'The Reverend Rigdum Rabelais'.

Unfortunately, the 1791 Report of the Commissioners was never implemented. It mirrored a great deal of Orde's work of a few short years before. Political events took centre stage; the French Revolution, the Act of Union of 1800, and there was considerable unrest in the Irish countryside, culminating in the 1798 Rising.

Orde's extensive plan for Irish education in 1787 came at a time when the political situation could not divert its attention from more immediate concerns. Education was not a priority at this particular moment for the Irish Parliament, and the Westminster Parliament had other fish to fry as well.

Orde's fourteen resolutions asked for a complete overhaul of education in Ireland, though Orde, one must mention, did not refer to the largest number of schools, known as pay schools or hedge schools, at any stage. As he wished for a system which would have as its fundamental tenets the values and beliefs of the Established Church, the popular pay schools, by their nature and affiliation with Catholicism were automatically excluded.

The Chief Secretary went into great detail in his fourteen resolutions; different types of schools to be revamped; lands to be procured for the erection of such institutions; it was imperative that the Lord Lieutenant, the Duke of Rutland be informed and addressed in such a fashion that plans could be initiated to get the show on the road as efficiently as possible. With that in mind, Orde had hoped to have the full plan be put into effect by the commencement of the next parliamentary session.

He was very concerned with funding his system, and with that in mind, he asked that an annual fund be made available at the discretion of the Lord Lieutenant:

> For the purpose of gradually building or purchasing, or otherwise providing proper schoolhouses, and conveniences annexed thereto, in every parish or union within the kingdom, in which they may be requisite, for the residence of the schoolmaster, and the free instruction of the poor.[20]

20 *Irish Parliamentary Register*, vol. 7, 496.

Parliamentary Reaction

The parliamentary response to Orde's plans was generally one of approval, but some members wished to have some time to reflect upon the details. One such M.P. was a Mr James Stewart, Killymoon,[21] County Tyrone, who felt the plan confined education in the middle and higher ranks to members of the Church of England.

In response, Mr Orde explained that nothing had been finalized at that particular stage:

> That he intended nothing final in the present session, relative to the system now proposed; his idea was, to have the resolutions passed through the committee, in order to enable him to have them printed; early the next session they might be taken up; and in the interval, gentlemen would have full time and opportunity to give them due consideration.[22]

Furthermore, Mr Browne of Trinity College, said:

> that he thought it unreasonable, if not haughty, to call upon gentlemen to give their assent, *infianter,* to a long elaborate detailed system of education – the subject was so important and so difficult, that it had occupied the mind of the proposer for two years.[23]

Browne expected to have enough time to speak with his constituents about the plan and get their views. He also felt aggrieved at the thought of having had no correspondence with Trinity about the proposed second university, and this tantamount to neglect which was 'a fresh instance of that disrespect which coxcombs from Eton and Westminster were too apt to show'.[24] He was not finished there, as he demonstrated his criticism of

21 *Irish Parliamentary Register,* vol. 7, 496.

22 *Irish Parliamentary Register,* vol. 7, 496.

23 *Irish Parliamentary Register,* vol. 7, 496.

24 *Irish Parliamentary Register, 1787,* vol. 7, 496. He also denied the superiority of the scholars of England in the sciences, and he denied their superiority in real substantial learning.

the proposed Provincial Schools, which he described as utopian. He also felt that the idea of a 'great school' would be hostile to morals:

> He was by no means satisfied that a very great school contributed much to learning – there are many schools in this kingdom, which produce excellent scholars. Unless he was much misinformed, boys at the great English schools are debauched at a very early age, and indeed, with all the fashionable vices to a degree scarce to be conceived.[25]

Browne further elaborated by accusing Orde of being mistaken in his ideas about the state of education in Ireland[26]:

> We are not such fops in learning as elsewhere. We are not so much accustomed to bring forward, in private company, a little smattering of quotation and general observation, as others do, to dazzle those who are not quite such great smatterers as themselves. Nor are we so much accustomed in public perhaps, to weave chaplets of false flowers, to crown our own heads, or to pronounce declamations on *Doctrina vim promovat infitam,* with as much pomp, as if our theme had been some newly discovered fragment of classic ore, and as if nobody had read Horace, till exotics came to teach it to us; but in solidity we were nothing deficient.[27]

He then went on to point out that those leaders of affairs in Ireland were bred here at home. Would Orde accuse these individuals of ignorance, Browne asks rhetorically, and why then had he said that 'for lack of learning the land perisheth'? And, Browne continued in a similar vein with his comment that Orde and other Englishmen were rather insulting to the Irish that they 'must teach us how to improve the education of the youth of the land, and the principal instructors of the rising generation here should not be thought worthy of being consulted'.[28]

At this point, the business of the House closed to resume the following morning, Friday 13, 1787. As was the case with Griffith and the amount of praise laid upon Orde, so too it was with John Hely-Hutchinson, who had one crib about the plan – the proposal for a second university. The Provost began by praising Orde's brilliant abilities, extensive information, or more

25 J. Giffard, *Mr. Orde's Plan ...,* 146.
26 J. Giffard, *Mr. Orde's Plan ...,* 146.
27 J. Giffard, *Mr. Orde's Plan ...,* 146.
28 *Irish Parliamentary Register,* vol. 7, 508.

to the point, knowledge, and great goodness of heart. He favoured Orde's Provincial and Collegiate Schools. Hely-Hutchinson felt that introducing another university would be detrimental to the existing one.[29]

Emulation was a favourite concept of Orde's and in the case of the second university it was no exception. He believed that a second institution should emulate Trinity College Dublin, but the Provost would not accept that scenario. Trinity had been doing very well and catering for the country's needs, and it had a city centre location where lodgings were readily available

Mr Molyneux of the Granard Borough, County Longford, was also very supportive of Orde's proposals, seriously defending Orde on the Charter schools issue, a subject on which Orde had been attacked by Sir Francis Hutchinson.

The Chancellor of the Exchequer came down very strongly on the side of Orde in the following statement. The Chancellor stated:

> … the full, clear, and able statement of the right honourable Secretary had made such an impression on the committee, that he was convinced they would be nearly unanimous if they were now called upon to decide …[30]

He finished his input pointing out that Orde was motivated purely as a result of his regard for the welfare of the Irish people.

Arthur Browne, M.P. for Trinity College, moved that the resolution that another university might be useful be amended by adding the words 'or might no'.[31] This seemingly innocuous amendment was defeated, and without any further remonstrance all resolutions were passed unanimously.

The Chief Secretary was circumspect in his whole approach to presenting a very detailed education plan for Ireland. Its likes had never been seen before, and with full awareness of its intricacies he was determined to avoid offending any particular party. Likewise, he was unlikely to present a programme which would not be feasible to put into practice. One of the perennial bugbears of getting an education system off the drawing

29 *Irish Parliamentary Register,* vol. 7, 499.

30 *Irish Parliamentary Register,* 7, 504.

31 D. H. Akenson, *The Irish Education Experiment,* 65.

board was the issue of finance, and Orde had made provision in various locations within the pages of his plan for fiscal responsibility. When he stood up on the floor of the House he made a gentle embrace of the members by stating that:

> I hope that some liberal and extensive plan for the general improvement of education will be matured for an early execution.[32]

On more than one occasion, the Chief Secretary placated his audience when they were concerned about one aspect of his plans or another. He assured the House that the expense which the state would have to bear as a result of implementing his plan would be offset by the returning benefits which should accrue. Orde had a great deal of financial acumen, stemming mainly from his former role as Secretary to the Treasury. This enabled him to be fully aware of the expenditures associated with financing an education system, and he always had in the mind the possibility of self-financing the whole project, or, at least to strive towards that aim. At no stage did Orde expect to rely solely on public financing of his proposed education project – he held it that the exchequer would not be expected to foot the entire bill of an education system, but that other sources would be employed in playing their part. Tithes, chapters, deans, bishops, public officers, private benefactors and parish clergy are some of those who would be expected to contribute to financing Ore's education system, especially the Parish and Diocesan Schools. The provincial Schools could be funded by the Incorporated Society. Funding for the Collegiate Schools may come from lands forfeited as a result of rebellion in the seventeenth century, which could be leased out or sold with the resulting profits being made available for the schools. Regarding the second university, the Chief Secretary felt that there would be a charge on the public purse in its early stages, but he had a plan:

> I have not been altogether disappointed in my researches, and I would thus far venture to risk the expression of an [sic] hope, that unless I am much mistaken in my idea of the nature and circumstances of the object I have in view, there do exist the

32 J. Giffard, *Mr. Orde's Plan of an Improved System of Education in Ireland*, 3.

> possible materials for a fund sufficiently ample to relieve you from the more immediate articles of expense, and to contribute in some degree to the future maintenance of these liberal establishments.[33]

Furthermore, he asked that the whole House 'do forthwith resolve itself into a committee ...'[34] Involving the 'whole' House was a very democratic act on Orde's part. He was adept at allaying the fears and concerns of parliamentarians, and was always open to suggestions and advice from them, and allied to that he made them aware that he favoured a piecemeal approach to implementing his plans rather trying it all at once. He never wished to be viewed as a single 'contriver of so extensive a scheme, and 'I therefore take this moment to urge an earnest solicitation for all the auxiliary council [sic] and support, which not only the members of this committee, but every wise and learned man of the kingdom may be induced to contribute towards its perfection'.[35]

The proposals the Chief Secretary laid before the House were meant to act as a fulcrum point about which the members could ruminate on their own reflections, and then, perhaps return to parliament with ideas of their own. Just in case there might be early opposition or complete indifference to his proposals, Orde took it upon himself very early in his speech to the assembled members to assuage any misgivings they might have, and, perhaps to mollify and appease any potential antagonisms. He opined:

> Although I shall propose to you some principles, which, I hope, may receive you're approbation for a general plan, I am not yet prepared to call upon you to give your ultimate sanction to the means of its execution.[36]

The *Irish Parliamentary Register* records only a handful of the three hundred members as having spoken to Thomas Orde's ground-breaking plan for Irish education, in the Irish House of Commons. Five speakers were in favour of the plan; a further two were disposed towards it, but with some reservations; the remaining three were somewhat critical of the plan. Be

33 J. Giffard, *Mr. Orde's Plan of an Improved System of Education in Ireland,* 106.
34 J. Giffard, *Mr. Orde's Plan of an Improved System of Education in Ireland,* 3.
35 J. Giffard, *Mr. Orde's Plan of an Improved System of Education in Ireland,* 22.
36 J. Giffard, *Mr. Orde's Plan of an Improved System of Education in Ireland,* 4.

that as it may, when the debating came to an end, and when it came to casting a vote in the House, all fourteen resolutions were passed, without dissension. Let it be noted that the most vociferous member was Mr Browne, of Trinity College, who embellished his contribution with several politically-charged remarks of a nationalistic nature. The handful of members who spoke either in favour of or against the resolutions found little support among the body of M.P.s. Aside from the concerns of the three major church authorities, and Orde's decreasing health, the road was quite open for the implementation of the plan of education in the second half of 1787. Caution became the optimum word during those last months. Credit is due to Orde during the closing days of his work as Chief Secretary, and at a time when his health concerns were amplifying. In a letter from the Duke of Rutland to Prime Minister Pitt, anxiety is expressed on the state of Orde's health:

> Mr. Orde's health has been sacrificed to his zealous exertions ... in the service of the public, where ... his diligent and conscientious exertions have not been useless. His conduct has, in no instance, been distinguished by any inclination towards objects of emolument, nor has he shown any aspiration after rewards.[37]

The Churches' Response

If Mr Browne's response was reactionary and heavy-handed, the Catholic Church's was more of a rejoinder or counterblast. In early 1788, Archbishop Egan of Tuam wrote to Archbishop Troy of Dublin:

> I have, on receipt of your most esteemed favour, written to the prelates of this province of Tuam. Our thoughts on Mr. Orde's scheme of education are that it is a deep-laid and hostile plan against the interests of the catholic religion. Nor is it to be supposed from motives of persecution: but from a political view of strengthening the hands of government, by increasing the members of the established church. For what other

37 Rutland to Pitt, 28 August 1787. Quoted in L. Namier and J. Brooke, eds, *The History of Parliament ....*

> can be the design in establishing protestant schoolmasters in every parish, to the exclusion, no doubt, of catholic teachers, and with so many inducements to the poor to send their children there: the youth will there be fitted for different employments, in which protestants alone are trusted, and all these motives will be carefully and artfully insinuated and displayed before their eyes.[38]

The above is a typical example of the language used over the centuries by the Catholic hierarchy when they wished to express disagreement with individual or government policy in education. Church and State rarely gelled amicably, and more often than not much rancour ensued between the two parties.

The late eighteenth century was a time when the Catholic Church in Ireland exerted its influence in a variety of areas of Irish life, most notably, in the traditional practices of the wake and the pattern; the regulation of marriage and sexual behaviour; the preservation of public order, particularly in relation to the activities of agrarian and other secret societies and of feuding local factions. Of central concern to Catholic Church teaching at the time was the relations between priests and people, particularly the state of ecclesiastical discipline, the training, origins and social status of the Catholic clergy, and the religious beliefs of the Catholic laity, with the way in which these were transmitted and reinforced by religious education and practice. The Catholic hierarchy simply viewed Orde's proposals for education reform as interference in Catholic education.

Another commentator, and often proclaiming himself to be an advocate of Catholic theology and politico-church policy, the Rev. Timothy Corcoran had a particular interest in matters educational, and the following sentiments, expressed in 1931, a time not long after the War of Independence and Civil War, in which Catholic Ireland was a powerful watch dog overseeing state policy in various shapes. As far as Orde's education Bill of 1787 was concerned, Corcoran claimed that its aim was to consolidate and strengthen the hold of the Protestant State and Church on the educational position in Ireland. There was to be a full reconstitution of all Protestant schools, and this with the obvious purpose of supplanting, if possible, the

38 Quoted by T. Corcoran, 'The Dublin Education Bill of 1787', *The Irish Monthly* LIX (August 1931), 499.

thousands of illegal popular Catholic schools that were rapidly developing all over the country.[39]

Perhaps, a brief interlude is necessary at this juncture to place Corcoran's reflections in context. Corcoran was referring to the native pay schools or hedge schools that catered for more school-going children than any other provider in the second half of the eighteenth century.

Ireland, at the time bore witness to the Penal Laws, legislation that was passed by a Dublin parliament over a period of about fifty years. Some of the laws concerned education, but many other aspects of everyday life as well. Dissenters (such as Presbyterians) and Catholics felt the brunt of these laws.[40] The legislation constraining the dissenter population was far less comprehensive than the anti-Catholic laws, but there were underlying common elements. One of the key pieces of legislation affecting dissenters' status was the test clause of 1704 which checked dissenter involvement in institutions of the state. Some attempts at Westminster were made regarding repeal of the test clause. Leeway was gained by dissenters when the Toleration Act was passed in 1719. Under this legislation dissenters had their educational and religious liberties recognized, and they retained the right to vote and to sit in parliament; however, they remained excluded from the magistracy. The threat of full enforcement of the test clause was a standing grievance among dissenters until 1780.

In educational terms, Catholics were not allowed to keep school or to teach in one, and they (the well-off Catholics) were forbidden to send their children abroad to be educated, or have them taught in their homes by Catholic tutors. The only schools allowed to operate under the law were Protestant ones, and all university education was forbidden to Catholics. In keeping with such a sentiment, the Catholic hierarchy opposed vigorously Orde's idea that clerical formation for the priesthood could be organized within the confines of Trinity College. One of the bishops, Boetius Egan

39 T. Corcoran, 'The Dublin Education Bill of 1787', *The Irish Monthly* LIX (August 1931), 499, 495–500.

40 Following the English Reformation and establishment of a state religion, dissenting Protestants, Quakers and Jews all suffered a degree of civil disabilities also.

of Tuam, described the proposals as 'a deep laid and hostile plan against the interests of the Catholic religion'.[41]

Members of the Established Church (Church of Ireland or Anglican Church), while constituting a minority population, monopolized political power: thus the term 'Protestant Ascendancy' was coined in the eighteenth century to describe the class at the top of the Irish social and political pyramid.

Protestant political power in Ireland did not always see eye to eye with Westminster, and to the English, Ireland was a colony whose primary purpose was to be of benefit to England – it was inconceivable that anyone could think otherwise. However, Protestant Ireland refused, for the most part, to accept that Ireland was a colony with its attendant attributes of inferiority and subordination. They preferred to view the relationship between the two islands as that of 'sister' or 'brother' kingdoms, while at the same time conceding 'elder sister' or 'elder brother' status to England, which included a slight element of deference.[42]

Much has been written about the pay schools, some of it romantic and picturesque, and often from a political and nationalistic point of view. The schools survived for over one hundred and fifty years, at least one still operating in West Limerick in 1900, seventy years following the introduction of the National School System. Places of destitution and squalor, but also places of hard-won learning, and very often learning for its own sake, which is probably the best epithet one can bestow upon these academies. As we have attested, these schools were omitted by Orde's plan for a national education scheme.

41 John T. Troy, *The Excommunication of the Rev. Robert McEvoy, Priest of the Dublin Archdiocese for Promulgating and Upholding Principles Established by the French Revolution* (London: Printed by J. P. Coghlan, 1798), 9.

42 See, *An Inquiry into Some of the Causes of the Ill Situation of the Affairs of Ireland* (Dublin, 1731); *Considerations on Several Proposals for Preventing the Exportation of Wool …* (London, 1741). For Ireland as a 'child', see John Fleming, *The Country Gentlemen's Letter to the Citizens of Dublin* (Dublin, 1749). See also, Thomas Bartlett, 'The Rise and Fall of the Protestant Nation, 1690–1800', *Éire-Ireland, a Journal of Irish Studies*, Summer (1991), 7–18.

The Catholic Church, while not always supporting the pay schools, also found it very difficult to encourage their flock to attend the state-sponsored schools. During the year 1787, when Orde made public his thoughts on a revamped education system for Ireland, the Catholic hierarchy remained strangely silent on the matter.

As Orde's replacement as Chief Secretary was no shrinking violet when it came to education policy, the Catholic hierarchy were roused from their slumber by Fitzherbert's continuing with Orde's ideas, and especially regarding investigations into education in Ireland. An immediate response came from Archbishop Troy of Dublin when he circularized his bishops to discover what their thinking on the subject was. Much to his delight, the responses he received back indicated very strongly that opposition to the plan was widespread, at least in the Leinster district. Bishop Daniel Delany, of Kildare and Leighlin, who had taken the motto *fortiter et suaviter* upon his consecration, compared the state's involvement in education to the 'wolf at the door'. He claimed that it represented a 'sinister, insidious and illiberal business of disingenuous aspect' which had as its object 'the utter extirpation of our holy religion together with the property of its possessors'.[43] Other responses from other members of the hierarchy were of a similar nature and construct. Bishop Caulfield, of Ferns, took the ultimate approach and stated that Catholics alone should be responsible for the education of Catholics, and in consort with other senior clerics, frowned upon the idea of Catholic seminarians attending Trinity College. Another member of the hierarchy, Archbishop Boetius Egan of Tuam was particularly fervent in his condemnation of Protestant interference in Catholic education (see letter to Troy above). Egan, a practical man, made a request that Catholics should respond with their own scheme, as a counter-balance to that of Orde.

Catholic authorities looked upon Orde's insistence on having the schools he was proposing populated by Established Church personnel with considerable dismay. A Catholic pamphleteer objected to the Chief Secretary's refusal to countenance religious instruction other than that of

43 Quoted by J. Kelly, 'The Context and Course of Thomas Orde's Plan of Education of 1787', *Irish Journal of Education ...*, 20.

the Anglican Church in his school system, and labelled it 'a barbarous penal law',[44] and on another occasion he described it as 'a gothic edict against the improvement of our rational faculties'.[45] With such strong Catholic dissension, it is no wonder that the post-April period of 1787 lacked any real tangible dialogue or even comment in the public arena. Giffard's version of Orde's April speech in the House of Commons, College Green was published in July, but this did nothing of any consequence to raise any heckles.

Presbyterians had also felt aggrieved at Orde's instance on the new scheme being so heavily weighted in favour of the Established Church. His plan received no greater acceptance than it got from the Catholic persuasion. Allied to Orde's plan the Presbyterians under the auspices of the General Synod of Ulster presented a petition on 14 February 1787 to the Irish Parliament seeking assistance in establishing an academy or academies for the education of their youth 'for the sacred ministry'. This school was needed because they had:

> Hitherto been obliged to send their sons abroad to be instructed at foreign universities, and at the hazard of their personal safety, at an increased expense, and a considerable annual loss to the nation .... The petitioners find that the expenses of such an undertaking must greatly exceed the ability of individuals, and that unless a support more ample and permanent than that which can arise from private subscriptions be obtained, they must despair of carrying their wishes into effect ....[46]

This would obviate the need for their young men to go abroad to study for ministerships in foreign universities. The Presbyterian Synod of Ulster did not wish to have a university college in the north of Ireland run by the Anglican Church. Instead they wished for a Presbyterian-run college, supported by government finances. This would satisfy their need to have

44 Quoted in J. Kelly, 'The Context and Course of Thomas Orde's Plan of Education ...', 20.

45 C. Brennan, *A Critical Review of the Bishop of Cloyne's Publication; with occasional remarks on the production of some other writers, particularly those of Trinity College, and on the conduct of the present ministry. Addressed to his Lordship, by an unbiassed Irishman – pseud. for Charles Brennan* (Dublin: Printed by John Chambers, 1787; Electronic version, Farmington Hills, Michigan: Thomson Gale, 2003).

46 *Irish Parliamentary Register*, vol. 7, 169.

their own pastors preparing their own young men for the Presbyterian ministry.

The Rev. T. Corcoran, in his typically redoubtable style, makes the following observation regarding the Presbyterian demand for a special institution in which their young men would be prepared for the ministry:

> But there were Presbyterians in Ulster. They had the audacity to ask for their share. They wanted Presbyterian schools, controlled by themselves. With completely Pecksniffian disdain, without even condescending to argue with such troublesome persons, the responsible minister brushed aside the Presbyterian claims. Mr. Pecksniff was in action long before Dickens.[47]

During the debate which ensued following Orde's speech in the Irish Commons, Mr Stewart of Killymoon took the opportunity 'of mentioning to the Right Hon. Gentleman, a petition he had the honour to present from the Presbyterian Synod of Ulster, respecting the education of their youth designed for the ministry;'[48] but as the House was so empty he said he would not, without the consent of the Right Honourable Gentleman, make any motion on the subject. 'Mr. Orde expressed a wish that the right hon. Gentleman would not at this time urge that business forward, in which Mr. Stewart acquiesced.'

On this occasion the House was asked to grant aid to the Synod of Ulster's request, but the motion was opposed by the Provost of Trinity, John Hely-Hutchinson on the basis that he felt that it would be best if the three main religious denominations, Presbyterians, Catholics and Anglicans received their education in the same seminaries, with a view to promoting harmony, avoiding discord, removing bias and prejudices, and extolling the virtues of each, but not at the expense of the other; this should lead to a stronger, but less aggressive kingdom. The Provost had his own institution in mind as the college to which all three denominations would attend, but his thoughts were rejected by the House.

47 T. Corcoran, 'The Dublin Education Bill of 1787', *The Irish Monthly* 59/698 (1931), 495–500. Seth Pecksniff was a character from a Dicken's novel called *Martin Chuzzlewit* – Pecksniff was unctuous and insincere to such an extent that his name became synonymous with hypocrisy.

48 Mr. Orde's Speech and subsequent debate, 149.

Interestingly, Orde had very similar views to those of Hely-Hutchinson, and one feels it could be opportune to deal with the Chief Secretary's views on mixed education, as expressed by Thomas Orde when:

> he expressed his respect for the dissenters, but mentioned his decided opinion against separate places of education for persons of different religious persuasions, for that such distinctions tended to disunite the members of the same community. He thought Protestant dissenters and Roman Catholics should be educated in the Same seminaries of learning, as fellow-citizens of the same state, interested in the happiness of each other, and in the general prosperity of their country; and that such a mode of training our youth, would remove prejudices, and promote the harmony and strength of the kingdom.[49]

It is remarkable that Orde, as we know, left an indelible mark on the landscape of Irish education, and its future. Bearing in mind his comments in College Green on 15 February 1787, we must admit that he foreshadowed what was ahead of Ireland regarding the mixed education principle. Both he and the Provost of TCD held that it would be best for multi-denominational practices to become normative rather than sticking with segregation; the Provost had a vested interest in having multi-denominational practices in operation in Trinity College, but Orde had no such interests; his reasons were genuinely above and beyond reproach; for the good of all concerned and for the good of the country.

A second attempt occurred on 20 May when Mr James Stewart moved to have the petition, which had been signed by 400,000 Presbyterians, referred to the Committee of Supply. This second attempt also failed to make any progress in parliament. With the failure of the Presbyterians, principally in the northern half of the country, to get the support they had hoped for, and with Orde in the middle of the debate on the Synod's petition, meant that Presbyterian support for Orde's plan of education for the island of Ireland was dwindling fast.

Colm McEvoy draws an interesting analogy between the Presbyterian situation in the 1780s and the manner in which they were the first to withdraw their support from the national school system in the 1830s. McEvoy

49 *Irish Parliamentary Register*, vol. 7, 170. Orde addressing the Irish House of Commons, 15 February 1787.

also reminds the reader that in a similar vein Archbishop Egan's retort to Orde's plan foreshadowed the MacHale response to the national system, and in particular the Stanley Letter. Interestingly, both bishops were representing the same archdiocese.[50]

For the Established Church interests, the situation was not as glowing as one may at first suspect. Oliver MacDonagh takes up an unusual historical interpretation in so far as the Established Church would suffer financially as a result of the reform. But, not only financially, it would include 'a diminution in the Church of Ireland's control of schools and an increase in "rational" teaching and the inculcation of "the principles of rectitude and beneficence into the hearts of the rising generation"'.[51]

Archbishop Robinson, Church of Ireland Bishop of Armagh, had some misgivings about Orde's proposals and he was reported 'cold, if not hostile to the whole scheme, except the proposal to situate a university in Armagh',[52] while the Bishop of Cloyne, Dr Woodward, was much more at odds with the proposals. He was made more extreme in his views by Whiteboy activity in his diocese, which he viewed as a Catholic attack upon Protestantism. With regard to the status of Protestantism in Ireland, Woodward 'was opposed to any attempt to alter the status of the Charter Schools and he used his not inconsiderable influence to counter their critics'.[53] Therefore, Orde's plan to extinguish the Charter Schools met with strong obstruction.

There were many members of the Established Church who favoured the Chief Secretary's proposals. Among them was Charles Agar, Church of Ireland Archbishop of Cashel, when writing to John Giffard[54] affirmed that the subject of education 'is of the first importance in every country,

50 C. McElroy, *Thomas Orde, 1746–1807: Educational Innovator* (M.Ed., thesis, UCD, 1994), 100n.

51 Oliver MacDonagh, *The Inspector General: Sir Jeremiah Fitzpatrick and the Politics of Social Reform, 1783–1802* (London: Croom Helm, 1981), 65.

52 See James Kelly, 'The Context and Course ...', 19.

53 See James Kelly, 19. The Whiteboy campaign was largely confined to the province of Munster, and it was not adverse to militant activity.

54 He, who was an employee of the Chief Secretary, and the person responsible for reporting on Orde's speech in the Irish House of Commons, 12 April 1787.

as on a proper system of education, suited to the different ranks of men, depend the morals of the people'.[55]

He went further:

> '... if the day be approaching when we shall see a well digested plan of education permanently established throughout Ireland I shall congratulate my country on having obtained one of the greatest blessings which providence can bestow on any people.' Though Agar was in favour of a comprehensive system of education for Ireland, he had some reservations about Orde's concept of a College of Visitors. He felt, also, that there was no need for the government to reform the diocesan schools as the bishops were quite able for the task. However, he wished, along with other senior clerics, such as Charles Dodgson, Bishop of Elphin, that Orde's plan be implemented.[56]

The graphic accounts of schools, especially the Charter Schools, of the likes of Fitzpatrick and Howard did not sit easily on the shoulders of some of the leading prelates of the Established Church, especially when one thinks of the responsibility Orde's plan would bestow upon the very same individuals, who would be expected to participate in widespread reform of the schools in their domain.

There were other aspects to Irish society which could confirm or disavow a buttressing of the Chief Secretary's plan.

The Reaction of the Press

On the evening of Orde's speech in the Irish House of Commons the *Dublin Evening Post* felt that the plan was agreeable, but had some regrets:

> ... it is not in our power to inform the kingdom that it is meant to include the Roman Catholics in it. That body will remain in as lamentable a state with respect to a mode of acquiring education as before. If it is really the wish of administration to render the substantial service to the kingdom by their system of education, they will certainly make some provision for the Roman Catholics of Ireland. Destitute

55 Bolton Manuscripts, Ms. 15,881/3.

56 James Kelly ..., 19.

> of any mode of acquiring education at home, they are forced to migrate for it to a foreign country ....[57]

And, the 'Post' did not stop there as it proceeded to elaborate on the plight of the Catholics of Ireland, claiming that they were criticized for their ignorance but laid the blame for this squarely at the feet of the Castle administration. In the editorial of the 'Postscript' the writer says that one might as well put out a man's eyes and then upbraid him for being blind as to impute ignorance to the Roman Catholics. Then it stated that it was the intention of the legislature (through Orde's plan) to remove the aforementioned 'ignorance', they must first remove the cause of which it was merely a consequence.

Despite much protestations, the newspaper was appreciative of Orde's work, and it defended him against those clergymen who found issues with his proposals. The paper also pointed out that a moral obligation rested on the shoulders of the clergymen who found fault with the plan:

> The idea of compelling the clergy to contribute towards the support of public schools under Mr. Orde's system, has struck many reverend gentlemen with fear and trembling. But as Mr. Orde very properly observed, poverty is not one of their complaints, and as they, of all others, should be forward in contributing to the establishment of a system whose sole objects are, to diffuse the principles of morality and religion; to humanize those whom ignorance has reduced nearly to the depth of barbarism, and impart as extensively as possible the blessings of education, it is to be hoped they will embrace the opportunity with cheerfulness and alacrity.[58]

That was April, but by August, the pitch had gone from a trickle to a cascade against the clergy:

> Many members of the Established Church feel actual trepidation at the very idea of Mr. Orde's plan of education. It will wrest from them those funds which were left by well-disposed persons for the promotion of knowledge, but which is now consumed in gluttony or avarice.[59]

57 *Dublin Evening Post,* 12 April 1787.
58 *Dublin Evening Post,* 19 April 1787.
59 *Dublin Evening Post,* 28 August 1787.

No doubt, the 'Post' was quite critical of the manner in which the extensive funds made available by such persons but was so ill-managed by the clerics of the Established Church. It takes one more swipe at the Church authorities:

> In many parts of the kingdom even those nominal schools are not preserved, although princely revenues are received by the incumbents, for the purpose of seminaries for the education of youth.[60]

Orde, naturally, was fully aware of the condition of the existing schools, and this was one of the principal prompts which injected vigour in the Chief Secretary soon after his arrival in Ireland. Having had significant time to digest the Orde proposition, for it was not cast in stone by September, when the 'Post', one again threw its weight behind the plan:

> From the outline we have seen ... we have not a doubt but this system will give universal satisfaction. To see this excellent plan carried into speedy and effectual execution is our earnest wish, as it must be of every friend to this country. It will go further to effectuate a reformation of manners, and towards the establishment of pure morality, than all the exertions of the clergy, since the days of St. Patrick.[61]

Take, for example, the phrase 'universal satisfaction' – a phrase Orde used many times, as did some of his ardent supporters. However, one has to be mindful of the underlying comments such as the one above. Orde was proposing a 'universal' plan of education for the whole country, hoping that once the first teacher was appointed to one of the 'Orde' schools everything would neatly fit into place and within a short period of time all the different religious denominations in Ireland would succumb to the enthralling wish bone that was placed before them. They would accept the Established Church school personnel, and happily be enamoured of the same church's teaching, in effect become Established Church citizens. This was expected of Catholics and Presbyterians, alike. This was happening at an exceptional level of gullibility, innocence and callowness. One would expect more from a Chief Secretary. It is difficult to know

60 *Dublin Evening Post*, 28 August 1787.
61 *Dublin Evening Post*, 8 September 1787.

to what extent he wished to introduce his plan piecemeal. That aspect needed to be well entrenched with all future participants, so that this enormous edifice that Orde was talking about would at least begin its life with a cornerstone, and then he could build his edifice, with some hope of success.

One of the reasons the whole concept failed to materialize began with the absence of discussions with religious leaders who were less likely to be supportive of the scheme than others. Orde should have written to the Catholic hierarchy, individually, explaining the most attractive aspects to them and, perhaps, how their flock might benefit.

The bulk of those parliamentarians who listened to Orde during his three-hour speech were not politicians, perhaps, in the strict sense of the word. None of them had to canvas for votes from door to door; all were wealthy, and unrepresentative of 'their' people; some could be described as the rotten borough brigade, while for most of them parliamentary duties was simply a part time chore. On top of that, the Irish House of Commons was little more than a dressed-up local authority, while mother Westminster was forever keeping a close eye on proceedings.

We all know that the period in question was one of political upheaval; on the one hand we had the American Revolution and one the other we had the French Revolution, which led a 'reign of terror' in the midst of the loss of the 'Devine right of Kings'. Ireland, too had notions of revolt, and though the country became united against the historical enemy, and formed into corps of United Irishmen, and with the remnants of a French fleet landing on the West coast to aid the rebels, nothing much changed, except Ireland joined Great Britain in 1801 and remained so until the Government of Ireland Act, 1920.

There seems to have been a shift in editorial policy within the offices of the *Dublin Evening Post* between April and September 1787, from initialling merely welcoming the plan as a generally sound approach to an education outlay for the whole country, to a very strong endorsement of Orde. There is a possible reason for this, and it hankers about the Presbyterian attempt to seek a separate entity in educational terms for themselves. This sectionalism did not quite fit in with Orde's unified Bill, and neither did the 'Post' recognize any value in it which would enable a unified education system fulfil its duty, as it were, in terms of a unified effort on Ireland's behalf. A general plan of education was preferable to a segmented one, and in some way this was in keeping with the political motivation which was rife in the country at the time. The paper went on to point out that:

> All religious sectaries without distinction will then have and easy and inviting opportunity of acquiring a liberal education. Besides, the idea of separately educating the youth of different persuasions is given up; as it must have a tendency to widen the distance between them, and to give rise to bigotry. By an universal intermixture of all religious and ranks, there will be no room nor leisure for speculative animosities; and this incorporation will also introduce the higher to the lower ranks, whom custom has long kept asunder.[62]

This was a complete exculpation for Orde' plan coming from a newspaper, which was a few months earlier finding loopholes in his proposals. One has to bear in mind the reality of the situation at the end of the eighteenth century where the majority of the nation's inhabitants could scarcely read. This was a situation in which one social class was providing a plan for an educational scheme, that at one level, was universal, but universal to what extent. Was Orde's system provided by people, many of whom were educated at some of the top universities in Britain, for a people, many of whom spoke a different language, and attended a local hedge school for a year or two, or more (and these were the ones who could afford to pay), and those who did not attend were unable to read? Perhaps, it would be fool hardy to over-estimate the power of the press at this particular time. Literacy in Ireland only made progress in the nineteenth century. However, the growth of literacy went hand-in-hand with the development of printing, and this was in a healthy state in the later decades of the eighteenth century. The numbers of publishers in educational printing also increased during this period and carried on into the nineteenth century. One such publisher was George Ewing and Edward Exshaw concentrating on publishing and printing books for children, and this organization operated from Dame Street in Dublin.[63] The general

62 *Dublin Evening Post,* 20 September 1787.

63 See J. Kelly, 'Educational Print and the Emergence of Mass Education in Ireland, c.1650 – c.1830', in J. Kelly and S. Hegarty, eds, *Schools and Schooling, 1650–2000: New*

percolation of educational print aided and abetted the progress and expansion of education in the later decades of the eighteenth century.

Another newspaper, the *Volunteer Evening Post,* which was a mouth piece of the government administration was, naturally enough, supportive of Orde's proposals. Its rather eulogistic tone is palpable in the following quotation:

> Mr. Orde's system of education does honour to his head and heart, and will endear his name to our latest posterity. Eventually it must prove of the greatest importance to this kingdom, which has been for so long clouded by ignorance and superstition. In fact there is not a nation in Europe which stands in more need of that improvement, which is the perfect object of our benevolent secretary, than Ireland ...[64]

Other Reactions

Apart from church dignitaries, who expressed mixed messages, and the *Dublin Evening Post,* which was generally favourable towards Orde and his plan, there were others worthy of note who had relevant observations to make. The Limerick Grand Jury, and its foreman wrote to Orde on 16 April 1787, and thanked him for the proposed system. John Ferrar signed the letter:

> [It was, he said] a system in which are blended an universal philanthropy, a liberality of sentiment, which when carried into execution, will cause the author to be remembered by future ages, not only as the friend of Ireland in particular, but the lover of mankind in general.[65]

Perspectives on the History of Education (Dublin: Fours Press, 2017), 44. The publication of children's books was a lucrative, high-volume activity.

64 *Volunteer Evening Post,* 14 April 1787.

65 Bolton Manuscripts, Ms. 15,881/6.

A most interesting document, in the form of a letter, written by Edward Tighe[66] to Orde in September 1787, under the pseudonym 'Melantius'[67] castigated the ordinary people of Ireland for their indolence and their filth, while those in the province of Ulster ensure that their children are working as spinners, weavers and at preparing the raw materials in factories. In the other three provinces the situation is far different. The writer gives us a long introduction whereby he comes to a conclusion that the lack of a proper education system is the cause of most of the social problems he has witnessed.

To that end, he is extremely impressed with Orde's plan for education in Ireland, to the extent that it should solve the bulk of the problems associated with a languid and torpid culture. He states:

> The deficiency of education no splendour can conceal, no station can supply; nor is there any person, however elevated his rank, who would not willingly relinquish some part of his envied pre-eminence to be numbered with the children of knowledge.[68]

The author continues in a similar vein heaping praise upon praise upon Orde's plan. He says:

> Your plans are great indeed, comprehending the happiness of millions, and of ages yet unborn, beginning with the child of the meanest and most unlettered peasant, and ending in such as by their successful toils in the best service of the public, (the training and forming of its youth) shall be entitled to the most honourable distinction.[69]

There is a bigger problem in Ireland, according to Melantius, and that is the contempt the people show for the laws of the land. Again, he asserts the importance of education in reducing that contempt.[70]

66 Edward Stearne Tighe, lawyer, writer, politician who represented a number of constituencies in the Irish House of Commons, including Wexford, Wicklow and Cavan. He was a member of the Presbyterian Church.

67 Edward Tighe was a commissioner of accounts (1771–1795). Under the pseudonym 'Melantius', he wrote two political pamphlets: *A Letter addressed to Mr. Orde upon the education of the people 1787* and *Letters addressed to Mrs. Peter La Touche ….*

68 Melantius, *A Letter Addressed to Mr. Orde, upon the Education of the People* (Dublin: Printed by P. Byrne, 1787), 1.

69 Melantius, 5.

70 Melantius, 11.

In his comments on Orde's plan for the parish schools, for example, he agrees wholeheartedly with the Chief Secretary when he intends reinvigorating the Act of Henry VIII:

> The beneficed clergy were obviously the persons to look to for a supply, when it was intended to instruct the illiterate not only in the English language, but in English Reformation. Would to God the clergy had made this work the chief object of their study; truth, industry, and honesty would then have filled the land.[71]

Melantius feels that there many social problems in Ireland, as we have alluded to, but, by far the biggest and most ruinous is the whisky and other spirits. He asks the government to abolish these drinks, and he clarifies his argument to some degree that the words, 'licensed to sell spirits" are words certain to disgrace and ruin a nation.[72] If the government, he claims, is unwilling to abolish spirits then it should increase the duty on spirits to five shillings per gallon. It was selling at the time for two shillings per gallon.[73]

By the time we reach page twenty-six of his thirty-nine-page letter, there is some mellowing in the air in so far that:

> [i]t is a mistake to conceive that the people of Ireland are by nature more lazy, more ferocious, or more cruel, than in other countries. Transplant them and the reverse of the assertion is more near the truth.[74]

Though he finds Orde's plan for Irish education very commendable, he expresses some doubts about its implementation if the government declines to take the lead in this enterprise. Consequently, no progress will be made without strong government guidance and support. 'Ireland', therefore, 'must be contented to remain the most dissimilar and motley nation in Europe; with this peculiar and extraordinary distinction, that the inferior orders of the people will be in this the most profligate and useless.'[75]

71 Melantius, 12.
72 Melantius, 19.
73 Melantius, 19.
74 Melantius, 26.
75 Melantius, 39.

Melantius also honed in on what Orde had to say about female education, and as is the case in other spheres, he agrees with the Chief Secretary when he says:

> I am ready to allow everything that can be advanced in favour of their superior innocence, but if they are not trained with greater care, (as their wit is generally sharper than that of men, and their attention less occupied) many of the evils complained of must remain.[76]

The document by Edward Tighe was the most positive for Orde and his plan of education in Ireland. Much of the letter, possibly sixty per cent is devoted to Tighe's campaign for the tightening of laws relating to the sale and consumption of spirits. He did, however, advance the cause of Orde's plan, though Orde by the end of 1787 had other plans in mind.

Orde and Edward Tighe, the author of the *Letter* rarely crossed swords, and some of the very poor in Ireland in the latter half of the eighteenth century engaged in chronic violence against Protestant tithes, land enclosures (by Protestant and Catholic landowners), and evictions, to such an extent that the former's plan for education should be systematic. This, he felt would ameliorate living conditions and kerb endemic bigotry and violence.[77]

On a broader level, a systematic education formula never boded well with British governments and the Catholic hierarchy, as neither of them wanted to propel dramatic change in Ireland. The Catholic Church primarily sought to thwart the so-called 'Second Reformation', a vigorous Protestant evangelical movement that peaked in the 1820s (but, began much earlier), and the British government aimed to keep Ireland in its proper place. The word 'systematic' is important here, as it is associated with being 'well-ordered', and in a country that was rife with underground agrarian organizations that was precisely what a ruling authority required in order to quell uprisings.

76 Melantius, 18.

77 O'Higgins, Laurie, '(In)Felix Paupertas: Scholarship of the Eighteenth-Century Irish Poor', *Arethusa* 40/3 (2007), 421–450.

Orde, on completion of his speech in the House of Commons, announced that he would now proceed with reading to the House his fourteen resolutions which would form the basis of an education bill.[78]

General Comment and Conclusion

He had sown a number of seeds, among them, the idea that educational planning needed to be firmly based on reliable data. It is true that Orde's efforts came to nil at the time of his attempted reform. However, it is reasonable to say that he was the originator of the notion of a plan of national education. He introduced the concept of 'children of all religious persuasions' going to schools, preferably the same local school. This was one of the cornerstones of the national system established in 1831. For example, one of the principles of 1831 refers to the need to admit 'children of all religious persuasions' to the newly proposed national schools. Orde's work was a yardstick in the development of the essence of ideas from which the national system of education was eventually to be devised.

In the short term, the Orde proposals came to nothing. However, over the next few years, and perhaps longer, they gave rise to an accelerated level of interest in Irish education. A great deal of research into education provision was undertaken, particularly regarding the state of schools. The four existing tiers of Protestant-run schools in Ireland were scrutinized, with depressing results. Hely-Hutchinson' designs of a revamped Irish education provision were made available to Orde prior to the latter's speech in parliament. Orde, though with indifferent health, gathered an unprecedented amount of evidence, including statistics regarding elementary, intermediate and tertiary education. Thus, by the time the 12 April 1787 came about Orde was well-versed in education matters giving almost a *carte blanche* to present a scheme which would mean a total restructuring of education in Ireland.

78 See Appendix A.

In many ways Orde was an unlikely reformer, as his early experiences of politics and administration saw him in Whitehall, and at the Treasury. In the context of Irish education in the 1780s and 1790s the Penal Laws are being revoked, which allowed for some increased Catholic and Dissenter freedoms and constitutional rights. Orde's plan for education was the most comprehensive, elaborate and aspirational in Irish history up to that time. Many members of parliament were impressed and duly supported the scheme. Reactions were generally overwhelmingly in favour of Orde' plan. Hely-Hutchinson supported the plan, but he held back on one aspect – a second university.

In the long run the plan failed to gain a foothold: Orde's sponsor, the Duke of Rutland died; Orde resigned from his position as Chief Secretary. The future of the plan depended on Orde's replacement as Chief Secretary, Alleyne Fitzherbert, who had an healthy interest in educational matters. Both the lord lieutenant, the Marquis of Buckingham and Fitzherbert were disposed to education reform, but not so much concerning Orde's finer details. The upshot was the appointment of commissioners to look into Irish education, in particular its schools. This appointment committed the new administration to nothing except it gave them time to assess the situation. As James Kelly states, it was a 'sensible holding position'.[79]

Orde had considered the education of girls at a time when female education did not feature prominently in educational endeavours. Likewise, he was keen on *mens sana in corpore sano* and made provision for such. His percipience and sagacity make it difficult not to consider Order as a significant contributor to the course of education history in Ireland.

A defective education system such as the one pertaining to Ireland in the eighteenth century needed someone like Thomas Orde, a person who displayed both commitment and initiative to transform the haphazard and ad hoc situation into a coherent whole where efficiency and efficacy would become key components. He envisaged a 'superior' Protestant education system for Ireland, and he saw his plan counter-balancing the meagre and, yet motley collection of schools, and providing a scheme which would be

79 J. Kelly, 'The Context and Course of Thomas Orde's Plan of Education of 1787', *Irish Journal of Education ...*, 22.

beneficial to all within the island of Ireland. And, for this system to work efficiently and with optimum effect a series of investigations would be undertaken from time to time in order to collect and collate reliable data. The state, of course, would now be granted a new role in education provision, as well as in inspection of schools.

However, with Orde's resignation the impetus was lost. Perhaps, he was too ambitious at a time when there was a regency crisis and the French Revolution could spill over across the channel causing unrest in a place like Ireland. The investigations following Orde's time found a location in the 1791 Report from the commissioners, though it was not published until 1857/8. Perhaps, the tide had begun to turn somewhat as two Catholics were appointed to the first Commission on Education Inquiry in 1791.

Due to the absence of a seriously well-judged commitment by the three main church bodies in Ireland to the Orde proposals put before the Irish House of Commons on 12 April 1787, a dead letter was in the offing. During the summer months of that year virtually no progress was made regarding the Chief Secretary's efforts to initiate a momentous education scheme for Ireland. In scope and vigour, it had no precedence. Orde brought a certain sense of vitality to the dialogue surrounding its initial introduction in the Irish parliament. However, no sooner had the Chief Secretary introduced his plan that his health deteriorated to such an extent that a replacement was in the ether in Dublin Castle. The press, in the shape of the *Dublin Evening Post,* was out of the blocks fairly quickly to announce that:

> Mr. Orde ... will resign his office as Secretary to the Lord Lieutenant of Ireland, on the close of the present sessions, in consequence of his ill state of health.[80]

When this was announced by the newspaper, the ink was hardly dry on the document he had produced in the Commons a few days before. And, by the beginning of Autumn, further comment by the *Volunteer Evening Post* added fuel to the fire of speculation in the corridors of power. Orde, however, was not ill enough to relinquish his duties just yet, as he dispatched John Reeves, an English legal writer, to Ireland, in a bid to undertake some work of preparation regarding the future implementation of Orde's

80 *Dublin Evening Post,* 17 April 1787.

plan. This meant that Reeves found himself touring the country, and meeting with interested parties, including clergymen of the Established Church. The attorney-general, John Fitzgibbon,[81] prepared a bill to legalize the sale of the lands forfeited during the seventeenth century and still in crown hands. These monies could be used in the establishment of the schools proposed by Orde. All the while, the Chief Secretary's day of reckoning was approaching, and coupled with that was Reeve's lack of achievement in procuring sites for schools, so that by the end of October he had returned to England, without having accomplished a great deal. About the same time, Orde's political sponsor, the Duke of Rutland died, and this gave vent to Thomas Orde's resignation.

Orde had been suffering from ill-health almost for his entire time in Ireland. In September 1786, we find the Duke of Rutland writing to the Prime Minister, William Pitt, and this is what transpired:

> I understand Mr. Orde is much recovered at Spa, so that I trust he will be able to resume his station in Ireland; but he must determine on that measure speedily, as the affairs and the detail of this country will render his immediate return of absolute necessity. It is wise, however, to be prepared against every possible contingency, and in the event of his wishing to decline, let me ask, whom have you in your view to recommend competent to succeed him, remembering I can have no general objection to any one immediately connected with you? .... Fitzherbert you have long known to be my friend, and that I wished originally to have engaged him, but the distance and delicacy of his situation, and the pressure in point of time, rendered it then an impracticable measure or idea; the same adverse reasons, I fear, may still remain.[82]

Rutland, later in the letter, reminds the prime Minister that at some time previously, two other names were mentioned regarding the Chief Secretary's post in Ireland. It is likely that this was 1784, when Orde was appointed, but the letter, unfortunately, does not name either of the two

81 John Fitzgibbon, one of a great number of lawyers who went over to the church of Ireland in the eighteenth century. He became a zealous defender of that church, and he was father of the future Earl of Clare, chief architect of the Act of Union.

82 Letter from the Duke of Rutland to Pitt, Blackrock, 13 September 1786. Available in, John Duke, *Correspondence Between the Right Honble William Pitt and Charles Duke of Rutland: Lord Lieutenant of Ireland; 1781–1787* (London: Forgotten Books, 2015), 162–164.

The Orde plan of 1787 was never implemented, and neither did it form the focal point of any parliamentary dialogue beyond 1787. There was a certain impulsion associated with Orde's plan, but with his resignation and departure from Ireland, that degree of incentive and motivation went with him. Fitzherbert, his successor, did not seriously push for the implementation of Orde's plan, but he did initiate an investigation into the state of education in Ireland. The resulting report, though a draft was ready in late 1788, was not published, nor was it presented to parliament, and it became known as the 1791 Report. It did not get the publication go ahead for almost seventy years.

An interesting slant on the whole affair by James Kelly is that Orde's plan was too elaborate, too extensive and its scope was so broad that it militated against its implementation. In fact the plan has never been implemented, nor, realistically could it have been. At the time, and later, one of the biggest issues which was immersed within the holy grail of Irish education the question of religious denominations. The pattern developed from being Protestant versus Catholic, to embrace all the other versions of Protestantism. In Orde's time the issue of proselytism was a bone of contention, and it could have been said by Catholic interests that his plan encouraged that policy. Notwithstanding the relationship between Catholic and Protestant, in Orde's time there was always a layer of attrition just below the surface of discourse. The Chief Secretary's plan, for that reason alone, **could not** have been implemented, as Catholic prelates would not support it, and even some Church of Ireland senior clerics would not support it. Likewise with the Presbyterians, who would not stand squarely with the implementation of Orde's proposals.

One could claim that Orde's educational planning approach, before he presented his report, was to set in train a similarly essential exercise in Irish education which was to have long-lasting results of benefit to those involved. Akenson and Milne have already certified that subsequent commissioners' reports had 'exhumed' the 1791 Report before they published their own. This was true of the *Commissioners of Education Enquiry, 1806–1812,* chaired by Richard Lovell Edgeworth. The link between the latter Report and the 1788–1791 document is palpable, and Akenson maintains that the 1806–1812 one was a revival of 1791 Report.[83] It might be plausible then, to assert that Orde was indirectly responsible for the fourteen reports

83 D. H. Akenson, *The Irish Education Experiment ...,* 74.

produced by the 1806–1812 commission. And, if that is so, the fourteenth report started in train a link which evolved all the way to 1831 when the national system was established. However, one must bear in mind that links between 1788–1791 and 1806–1812 can be putative, but links between 1791 and 1831 are certainly implausible, or at least dubious. There is one aspect of Orde's ideas and those of Stanley and Wyse which alludes to the 'mixed' education principle. This link is much more than tenuous, and it refers to 'children of all religious persuasions' attending the newly-created national schools in the 1830s. Another link may well exist between Orde and Stanley in that both of them wished for local contributions for the upkeep of schools in order to alleviate the burden on the exchequer. Also, both the Kildare Place Society schools and the national system took up Orde's plan for 'visitors'.

It is interesting to note that the Orde scheme to set up a 'Lord Lieutenant's School Fund' was put in place in 1819 under the auspices of the Kildare Place Society. And, Akenson informs us that 'up to 1848 the commissioners of national education drew their money from the Lord Lieutenant's education fund'.[84]

Orde wished that the Established Church should have a pre-eminent place in the running and control of Irish education. In his plans, he disregarded the people's schools, the Hedge Schools, which at the time catered for more students than any other provider. He did consider female education at a time when it was not commonplace to do so. In like manner he drew attention to the importance of physical education. On those two issues alone, the Chief Secretary proved himself to be innovatory.

84 D. H. Akenson, *The Irish Education Experiment …*, 126.

CHAPTER 5

Orde's Plan: Overview and Conclusion

Thomas Orde made two attempts to introduce a bill in the Irish House of Commons for the advancement of education. The second of these included a three-hour speech in the said parliament on 12 April 1787, which according to R. B. McDowell, 'in scope and detail was worthy of Pitt himself'.[1] Lecky, on the other hand, grudgingly admits that Orde's contribution to events in parliamentary history should not go amiss – 'it was not', he says', among the least memorable incidents …' in that parliament.[2] D. H. Akenson, on the other hand finds very laudable content in Orde's contribution to parliamentary debate on the subject of education:

> Orde's work was a touchstone in the evolution of the core of ideas from which the national system of education was eventually to be fashioned. Orde was the first legislator to realize that Ireland's educational institutions should be treated as a system, rather than as a collection of schools. This system, he believed, should not be limited to the middle and upper classes but should also extend to the teaching of the peasantry. Orde's plan implied the provision and control of schools by the central government. And narrow though Orde's religious prejudices may seem to the modern observer, his plan deserves notice for postulating that any state system of education should be open to all Irish children irrespective of their religious affiliations.[3]

Orde's involvement with and promotion of Anglo-Irish commercial enterprises took up much of his time, and this was in conjunction with his duties as Chief Secretary. It is surprising that he found space in his life for

1 R. B. McDowell, *Ireland in the Age of Imperialism and Revolution, 1760–1801* (London: Clarendon, 1979), 93.

2 W. E. H. Lecky, *A History of Ireland in the Eighteenth Century*, vol. II (London: Longmans, 1902), 514.

3 D. H. Akenson, *The Irish Education Experiment* (London: Routledge and Kegan Paul, 1970), 68.

an investigation of education provision in Ireland, but not only that, he also produced a thought-filled speech in the Irish House of Commons in College Green. This speech was published by J. Giffard a short while later. Unfortunately for the Chief Secretary, he was be-devilled with ill-health, particularly through 1786 and 1787. His indifferent health, along with the demise of the Duke of Rutland at the age of 31, his sponsor and supporter, fused together to bring about his resignation from Irish affairs. Orde was convinced that Ireland with an array of schools of various denominations, from basic elementary schools up to university level, but there was no coordinating body, no central administration, no inspection system to ensure that standards were uniform throughout the country. In the existing schools there was virtually no place for female pupils or students: we could excuse that by claiming it was society's expectation that such a situation would remain so. However, Orde had other ideas regarding female education.

His plan included an all-enveloping curriculum, from the classics to hand work, from the practical to the theoretical. All were welcome to participate in his scheme, and benefit from it. Circumstances, however, did not allow for this plan to take root; it never got beyond the three-hour speech in the House of Commons in College Green. Some supported his plan, while others, such as the Churches, found it wanting. It would appear that Orde had a sincere and genuine reason to alleviate the condition of the Irish people. He had a very difficult task on hand as half the population could not speak the King's English, and his plan did not cater for those whose language of communication was the vernacular only.

As Antonia McManus brings to the fore that it was through education that the Irish would be socialized and politicized along loyal, law abiding lines.[4] Orde was fully aware of this: he was clear about the moral qualities sought in the teacher and the bilateral nature of his duties to the child, intellectual and moral:

> He should be chosen with serious care in respect of morals and propriety of conduct and should not only be competent to impart the ordinary subjects of instruction,

4 A. McManus, *The Irish Hedge School and its Books, 1695–1831 ...*, 237.

> such as reading, writing and common arithmetic, but to inculcate also by plain and simple method the first principles of honesty, truth and industry.[5]

The insistence here on a strong sense of morality in a teacher became almost a catch word during the nineteenth century in Ireland and Britain, and in many continental educational settings.

Not only should the teacher be chosen with great care, but he should be of the Protestant persuasion. His insistence on this could well be at variance with his ideas on universal education without any difference being made for religious affiliations. In Ireland, this was a particularly strong issue, especially when the state, going back to Tudor times, did not provide for the education of those beyond the Anglican faith.

Orde had a preceptive curriculum in mind so that in future Ireland may well move away from 'all the violent and atrocious acts which had too often disgraced this nation'. Once the general basics of reading, writing and arithmetic had been well-established the schools would then concentrate on developing each boy's skills and knowledge in his own field of interest.[6] The curriculum on offer was quite extensive, including navigation, mercantile knowledge, modern languages, trade manufacturing, mathematics, geometry, architecture, drawing, husbandry and agriculture.

He saw education as a means of infusing 'the balm of information into the wound of ignorance'. He argued that Catholic participation in his proposed plan for a Protestant education system would surely disperse 'the mists of ignorance' and encourage Catholic appreciation 'of the superiority of our own (Protestant) doctrines'.[7] Orde was not original in his plans for Irish education. Lord Shelburne, the former prime minister, and John Hely-Hutchinson, Provost of Trinity College, Dublin influenced Orde prior to his pronouncements in 1787. Hely-Hutchinson had

5 John Gifford, *Mr. Orde's of an Improved System of Education in Ireland Submitted to the House of Commons, 12 April 1787 with the Debate Which Arose Thereon* (Dublin, 1787), 33. Quoted in Joseph Doyle, *Model Schools-Model Teachers?: A Nineteenth-Century Irish Teacher-Training Initiative* (Kilkenny: Geata Buidhe Books, 2020), 17.

6 C. McElroy, 'Thomas Orde and Educational Innovation, 1786–1787', 157.

7 D. H. Akenson, *The Irish Education Experiment: The National System of Education in the Nineteenth Century* (London: Routledge & Kegan Paul, 1970), 59.

completed his 'Outlines of a Great Plan' with a critical look at state and endowed schools. Colm McElroy, in his refreshing article 'Thomas Orde and Educational Innovation, 1786/87' is in no doubt that Hely-Hutchinson's 'Outlines' acted as a catalyst on Orde and his plan for Irish education. Hely-Hutchinson highlighted in his writings on education the numerous deficiencies in the existing education system. He pointed out to Orde that the Royal and Diocesan schools need financial investment, and the Charter schools needed to be looked at. He showed a genuine desire to improve the lot of the Irish people. He felt that the education should be extended to all parts of the community. The idea of upward social mobility may be discerned in the thinking.

He spent much of the winter of 1786 formulating his fourteen resolutions to be laid before the House of Commons, in the Irish Parliament, 12 April 1787. And, in April of the same year, 1786, Orde intimated very strongly his intentions regarding the cause of education in Ireland. In keeping parliament abreast of his thinking, on 6 April 1786, he outlined his objectives with regard to education provision; it should be extended universally throughout the country; it should be cheap; and very few would be excluded from his plans. One year later, by which time he had developed his ideas further on education, though still not entirely ready to implement, Orde put forward his grand plan for a complete restructuring of the Irish provision, at five levels. On this occasion, his presentation in the House of Commons in College Green was little more than an opening salvo in order to engender considerable debate among his parliamentarian colleagues.

We must bear in mind that Orde was referring only to the advancement of Protestant schools in Ireland, and to that extinct we must find fault with his plan. In many ways his plan was a denominational one even though he was critical of denominational education. Establishing schools for a minority population and expect the majority to attend was unrealistic to contemplate. The irony should not go unnoticed.

By the time Orde arrived in Ireland in 1784 there existed a motley collection of educational institutions, many of which had come into being on a distinctly ad hoc basis. Certainly, Ireland was without a system of education, as was the case in Britain and continental Europe. Altogether those schools catered for fewer than 14,000 pupils. Of these approximately

13,000 received a primary education while fewer than 1,000 attend secondary institutions.

Alongside this Protestant 'public' sector education was the Catholic 'private' sector, the Hedge Schools (Pay Schools) which catered for the vast majority of Irish children of school-going age. It was the Chief Secretary's belief that if state schools could be made efficient and available possibly some Catholic children might be enticed away from the Hedge Schools. Not that opening those schools to children of all persuasions was as liberal as it first seemed, for Orde believed that children who were maintained and educated at state expense should be brought up in the established religion. Once the basics were taught the schools should concentrate on developing each boy's skills and knowledge in his own field of interest. He was anxious that an immediate start be made in this area of provincial schooling and suggested that an operation could commence forthwith at New Geneva in Co. Waterford. The entire school might consist of 800 or 900 scholars. It would cost £12,000 per annum.

Much of the credit for stimulating debate on Irish education in the latter decades of the eighteenth century must go to Orde, and he used his high office as a springboard from which to propel his convictions. In presenting a proposed plan of education for Ireland to parliament in 1787 he debated the value of education as an agency of social reform in a way that was in keeping with radical ideas of the day. 'He imputed "all the violent and atrocious acts which had too often disgraced this nation" to a want of education and consequently to a want of obedience to the laws.'[8] Orde's scheme was never implemented, but it had the effect of focusing the attention of subsequent governments on the question of Irish education. He was responsible for initiating several educational investigations, beginning while he was in office, but continuing for many years following his departure from Irish shores. In March 1788, his successor Alleyne Fitzherbert moved for a commission to be set up to inquire into the funds for the endowment of schools. It was further to inquire into the condition of such schools, and to make recommendations for the improvement of education for the youth of Ireland.

8 Akenson, *The Irish Education Experiment*, 63.

Both the existing Parish and Diocesan Schools were ostensibly established during Tudor times to advance English cultural, religious, social and political interests in Ireland. These schools had failed to consummate the liaison established by Henry VIII and Elizabeth I, and the people. A variety of legislative efforts ensued in the seventeenth and early eighteenth centuries, but nothing worthwhile came of these attempts at introducing an adequate network of schools that would satisfy those who were behind these efforts. That all of the existing schools were ever near accomplishing their objectives was very unlikely, as they were few in number, such low numbers of pupils attended them, as well as the Catholic understanding that these institutions were little more than proselytizing advocates. Orde, as it were, had a *tabula rasa* upon which to mould his version of a revitalized system of education, and he duly set about the task with some measured gusto. His health was poor, and as it turned out he did not have much time to complete the task. This was a task which had nothing directly to do with his position as Chief Secretary, but his personal interest in education as a vehicle to improve people's lives had enabled him to embrace it wholeheartedly.

His insistence on probity when it came to funding his enterprise was of paramount importance. He declared:

> I could point out to you an immediate instance of glaring notoriety, where the funds assigned for the institution of schools compared with the employment of them, and the abuse of even the ostensible establishment of them, must upon every principle and common sense, be convertible to efficient purposes of public utility. The legislature has not only a right, but is bound in duty to act as a trustee for the public, of an abdicated or an usurped benefaction to their use.[9]

He was a genuine advocate for education reform in Ireland, albeit with an overt Church of Ireland bias. While he did not obviously advocate proselytism, his 'plan was in large measure a reflection of traditional Anglican thought on education'.[10] And, not only that, he favoured English staff, where feasible, in the schools he was proposing. His 'education for all'

9 Mr Orde's Speech, 92.

10 Atkinson, *Irish Education ...*, 67.

plan was probably very besmirched by the fact that in a practical sense, the largest population cohort, the Catholics, were left out of his proposals. It is a mysterious phenomenon that Orde did not foresee that omission as a stumbling block to his, otherwise, excellent scheme. He favoured a centralized system of education, with a permanent committee of the Privy Council to advise the Lord Lieutenant on concerns relating to educational matters. This, he claimed to be better than leaving decision-making to the whim of individual schoolmasters.

Hely-Hutchinson's plan for Irish education formed the basis upon which Orde cultivated his proposals, and in the mutual promotion of Ireland as a location for a complete national system of education, each had elements of virtuosity, mingled with the occasional need for secretarial refinement. Orde, of course, as we have seen, never wished to run headlong with his project into a situation without first of all declaring that each strategic embrace was attained. In all this, the Provost's plans for Irish education unleashed a mild catalyst in Orde's mind, and he dealt with it in a controlled manner in the House of Commons in College Green. Orde was very appreciative of Hely-Hutchinson's contribution to the project. His three-hour speech, followed by a long discussion with members of the House, must have impressed those who witnessed and partook in the occasion.

Apart from the earlier Tudor attempts at legislation, Orde was the first to recognize the importance of having a legislative underpinning for a system of education in Ireland. In fact, his bill was a bid to revitalize Tudor education Acts, but with a contemporary flavour: this meant having a school in every parish, a secondary school in every diocese, two great academies, a feeder school for university education and a second university. His plans also included a very innovative factor in that he provided for female education, something that was unprecedented. Orde had considered the education of girls at a time when female education did not feature prominently in educational endeavours. Likewise, he was keen on *mens sana in corpore sano* and made provision for physical education. His percipience and sagacity make it difficult not to consider the Chief Secretary as a significant contributor to the course of education history in Ireland.

A defective education matrix of schools such as that pertaining to Ireland in the eighteenth century needed someone like Thomas Orde, a person who displayed both commitment and initiative to transform the haphazard and ad hoc situation into a coherent whole where efficiency and efficacy would become key components.

His plan was innovative and all-encompassing from an administrative point of view; his inclusion of a provision of a College of Visitors, who would act as school inspectors, was ahead of its time. A precedent was set for school inspection by the Kildare Place Society in 1818, about thirty years following Orde's proposals. Perhaps, as Kelly points out, the extent and scope of his plan militated against its implementation.[11]

The assessment of his contribution to the history of Irish education can be measured by realizing the two-fold nature of his premise. He used his high office to investigate the existing provisions for education in Ireland, and then, and only then did he proceed to seek to implement a systematic scheme for a five-tier comprehensive outline, but with a legislative foundation. His insistence on a legal foundation for his plans pre-empted Thomas Wyse's concerns over the importance of a legislative footing in an education system by a half-century. It is important to note that in his provisions for a graduated five-tier system, the Chief Secretary was very eager to ensure that one's ability, rather than one's station, came to the forefront in his plans.

The two areas – research and legislation – are essential components of Orde's *raison d'etre* for his proposals. It was from these twin bedfellows that his scheme radiated outwards, and though the 1831 national system of education did not have a legislative basis, this should not detract from the import of Orde's unprecedented detailed contribution to the development of education in Ireland.

Orde's time in Ireland coincided with a great deal of social instability, with agrarian unrest very much intertwined in the everyday lives of ordinary people. That reality, coupled with Orde's propensity to view the purpose of education as a mechanism for quelling such agitation and unrest, was ideally placed to intervene with his graduated system of education,

11 James Kelly, 'The Context and Course of Thomas Orde's Plan of Education of 1787', *The Irish Journal of Education* 20/1 (1986), 3–26, 24.

'providing distinctive facilities for the main groups in the community,[12] and thereby establishing stability.

Once Orde vacated the office of Chief Secretary, the Irish Parliament never discussed his plans for Irish education. This may have been due to the regency crisis of 1788 when George III suffered from a temporary fit of insanity,[13] or it may be simply that the momentum was lost in the absence of its promoter. Coupled with that, it seems that nobody else in the House had the wherewithal nor the penchant for a project of somebody else's conception. There was also a strong crusade against his plans by the Church bodies, but especially the Catholic Church hierarchy. It seems that the Catholic Church had a perennial matter of contention with education being associated with the state; later, we see instances of that following the Synod of Thurles in 1850, and later still, we encounter an outrageous condemnation of the McPherson Bill in 1919.

Orde subscribed to the view that the central state intervened only to shore up the privileges of the Church of Ireland, and beyond this there was little compunction on governments to advance any further educational theories that would display any effective initiatives. The system Orde wished to introduce to Ireland was a safe one, the foundations already being in place in one form or another. He was the architect of an historical blueprint, and all it needed now was a model to match current requirements. In so far as his plan was watertight, he felt he had nothing to fear from church bodies or other organizations or individuals, but he did not countenance the reactions his proposals received, least of all from the Anglicans, the one religious denomination he set out to favour in the first instance. Orde had placed the Established Church in pole position in his new education system, but he failed to anticipate their response. He also failed to understand the attitude of the Catholic Hierarchy, who were always steadfast in claiming a position of derring-do in their dealings with other denominations and education matters. The ardour, dedication and integrity which Orde brought to the education debate in Ireland was less evident in government circles

12 N. Atkinson, *Irish Education: A History of Educational Institutions* (Dublin: Allen Figgis, 1969), 65.

13 A. McManus, *The Irish Hedge School and Its Books ...*, 39.

following his departure. His legacy was one that subsequently bore fruit, albeit in the fourth decade of the nineteenth century.

It would be wrong to assume that Orde's proposals in College Green, did not have implications for the future of education in Ireland. Perhaps, Akenson puts it very clearly when he declares that:

> Thomas Orde's educational legacy was not limited to the expression of new ideas which parliament promptly forgot; he was chiefly responsible for setting afoot a series of educational investigations that continued in progress and influence long after he had resigned as Chief Secretary.[14]

His ideas concerning standards both for teachers and pupils, the setting up of departments in schools, the establishment of an inspectorate, the need for a Lord Lieutenant's fund for Irish education – all these were ideas which were adopted in the future. We must recognize the traces of his finger prints on Stanley's Letter of 1831, especially with regard to Orde's belief that education provision should be universal, irrespective of gender or religious denominations. Taking account of these ideas of Thomas Orde and considering his perspicacity and zeal, it is difficult not to believe that the Chief Secretary's contribution in the field of Irish education was noteworthy and considerable.

His vision encompassed an historic inclusion of all parties within a legally bound framework, but his preoccupation with placing the tenets of the Church of Ireland at the pinnacle of his proposed system would have caused many internecine squabbles had his proposals been accepted. However, he was decades ahead of Stanley and Wyse who, in the 1830s, found a way to introduce a national system of education, though their scheme could not compare favourably in scope with that of Orde's.

14 D. H. Akenson, *Irish Education Experiment ...*, 68.

Orde-Postscript: Schools and Verdict

Diocesan Schools certainly did not improve as a result of Orde's labours. The Hely-Hutchinson report of 1791 revealed that there were eighteen of these schools, catering for a total of 324 pupils. By 1809 the number was down to seventeen, of which only eleven had their own separate school-houses. One of these was in a ruinous state; another begun twelve years earlier had never been finished; a third was only a thatched cabin; and in all, they only catered for thirteen free scholars out of a total enrolment of 432. In fact, one school had only one student whilst another had only six.

The Royal Schools too suffered from corruption. Godkin speaks of various abuses which were clearly not diminished as a result of Orde's plan. He tells us, for example, that the school at Armagh should have had an income of £1,043 in 1825, but in reality was in receipt of only £461. The situation was similar in Dungannon, whose income was being plundered 'to the extent of £500 or £600 a year'. The estates connected with the Royal Schools consisted of 13,627 acres in the north of Ireland. The administration of the funds was vested in the archbishops and bishops of the Established Church. According to Godkin:

> The church held it as her own private patrimony: and the Catholic population regarded it as part of her ample resources used for political and sectarian corruption. In 1782, there were in all the Royal Schools only thirty-eight free scholars; in 1835, notwithstanding the increase of the population, the growing demand for a superior education, the numerous parliamentary investigations, and the rising power of an enlightened public opinion, they had dwindled down to twenty-three.[1]

Godkin complained that charges in these schools were as high as those of first class private boarding schools, the average being thirty-five guineas for boarders, and eight guineas for day scholars.[2] His final comment on

1 J. Godkin, *Education in Ireland,* 41.
2 Godkin, 42.

the Royal Schools is a damning indictment: 'There is no efficient control over these schools .... There are no local committees, no adequate superintendence.'[3]

As for the Charter Schools, much evidence exists to show that improvement did not take place in these establishments in the latter part of the eighteenth century or in the early part of the nineteenth. Inspections were undertaken by, amongst others, Howard and Fitzpatrick. Howard was a prison reformer who visited Charter Schools in 1784 and again in 1787; Fitzpatrick, the inspector general of prisons, visited twenty-eight of them in 1787 – both men gave damning evidence on these schools before a committee of the Irish House of Commons formed in 1788 to investigate Irish education. A vigorous campaign to discredit the work of Howard and Fitzpatrick was carried out by the Incorporated Society and their friends in the Established Church, with the result that 'the Charter Schools continued pretty much undisturbed with little other than minimal changes in personnel and cosmetic physical improvement'.[4]

It is demonstrable then that none of the schools which Orde wished to reform changed as a result of his endeavours. Or is it? Certainly, if we are to take the uncritical view that his achievements are measurable in the way attempted here, simply by comparing the 'before' and 'after' states, then that would seem to be the case. However, such a view is surely simplistic. Orde did not operate in a vacuum. He was certainly a man of his times, blinkered in some ways by tradition. This may account for his insistence that his proposed new schools be run by the Established Church. It may also account for his disregard of hedge Schools. However, we must also consider the innovative side of Orde's design.

Orde had insisted on considering education for girls in an age when the young female populace was virtually ignored from an educational standpoint. Similarly, he had emphasized the importance of physical education. His approach regarding the importance of gathering statistical evidence to ascertain the extent of a problem before attempting to rectify it was one adopted by many later Chief Secretaries and commissions. His

3 Godkin, 42.
4 James Kelly 20/1: 23–24.

ideas concerning standards both for teachers and students, the setting up departments in schools, the need for an inspectorate, the desirability of establishing a Lord Lieutenant's Fund for education – all these were ideas which were adopted at some time by those coming after him. We have already seen traces of his influence on the direction taken by Stanley and Wyse on the circumstances surrounding the setting up of a National System of Education in 1831, especially with reference to Orde's belief that the educational system should extend to the teaching of the peasantry, irrespective of their religious affiliations. Taking account of these ideas of Orde and considering his perspicacity and zeal, it is difficult not to believe that the Chief Secretary's contribution in the field of Irish education was noteworthy and significant.

Verdict

Orde's plan, influenced by Hely-Hutchinson's, was significant as it represented the shift of emphasis in the use of education which, instead of attempting to proselytize or subjugate children, was aimed at the improvement of knowledge and behaviour, with the education system as 'the foundation for the superstructure of the state', which meant that improving the system would 'render that foundation not only more beautiful, but more secure and permanent'.[5] This was representative of liberal governments' growing concern with the security of economic and social development in the country. The state's rationale had shifted to the attempt to frame the population in apparatuses of security, which had the purpose of defending the population with police and armies, but also included institutions to secure economic and social processes as health, welfare and education.[6] Those individuals, who at the closing decades of the eighteenth century had plans for an education system in Ireland – Orde,

5 Mr Orde's Speech, 14.

6 Leon Tikly, 'Governmentality and the Study of Education Policy in South Africa', *Journal of Education Policy* 18/2 (2003), 162–165.

Bentham, Edgeworth – fitted the bracket of Tikly's description of the requirements of health, welfare and education. The end of the century witnessed a philosophical move from the age of proselytism to one of general welfare improvement for all citizens, including the lower orders. This was a noteworthy agenda which viewed the rights of the many having a place at the decision-making table as much as the elite in society.

Orde's plan for education in Ireland, despite his insistence on his scholars being brought up in the Established religion, did on occasions override contemporary associations with a class-based structure in society. He stated:

> The capacity for literary improvement is not confined to superior rank of birth alone, but ought to be cherished wherever it may be found or shall present itself, by encouragement and provision for its cultivation, and by honour and reward for its maturity. Incitements to competition, although different in their kinds, must conduce greatly to the progress of learning, both among the rich, and those of more humble situations; [the latter] to advance themselves to share in the higher objects of ambition.[7]

It is an important moment as it represented the shift in mentality of policy of the British state from the use of education as a disciplinary measure on the body of a child (to reduce criminal activity or proselytize individuals) to the incorporation of education in the gradual governmentalization of the state that extended beyond the institute and aimed at shifting the behaviour of a population, the creation of self-regulating citizens.[8] The effects of the Enlightenment on education, turning it into a serious professional study,[9] were seen throughout the plan with a heavy emphasis on science instruction and the improvement of teaching methods, which included the proper distribution of space and duties within schools.[10] Empiricism, rationalism and emancipation were fundamental aspects of in radical educational thought and gave logical underpinnings to many

7 Mr Orde's Speech, 80–81.

8 David Nally, '"The coming storm": The Irish Poor Law, Colonial Biopolitics, and the Great Famine', *Annals of the Association of American Geographers* xcviii/3 (2008), 714–741; 723–724.

9 Norman Atkinson, *Irish Education: A History …*, 64.

10 Mr Orde's Speech, 53.

radical educational ideologies. This was, of necessity, of theoretical import, such as that in Orde's plan, and it was difficult to counteract rote learning, indoctrination and authoritarianism, with an enlightened emancipated input to the child's environment in a school. Radical reformers, while embracing Enlightenment views, by preaching human freedom and intellectual development, met with school authorities more concerned with social control, moral conformity and political acquiescence than emancipation.

This was fundamentally the beginnings of a professional approach to teacher preparation, school management in proper school buildings with the necessary equipment to enable both teacher and learner undertake their respective duties. It was an new and exciting time for education in Irish classrooms, but it did provoke considerable controversy, a controversy that was never too far from the surface.

Appendix: Part of Orde's Speech on 12 April 1787

The system, which I would propose, should be extended in its benefits to all parts of the community. It should begin with the lowest ranks of the people, and ascend in different gradations to the highest, and tend to qualify the youth of each order for excellence in the stations and pursuits belonging to each. It may do more. It may give to the youth of every class an opportunity of bringing out and improving talents, with which nature may have endowed them, fitted to a rank superior to that which fortune had allotted to them. The preservation no less than the immediate encrease[sic] of learning may thus be ensured by the formation of more able instructors to future generations. It must be of material consequences to establish the uniformity and steadiness of sound discipline throughout the whole system. The safety and success of such a measure must not be put to the hazard of capricious or unconcerted changes and variations. The courses of study also, and occupations of the children, which should be settled with great care and precaution, ought not afterwards to depend for their observation upon the arbitrary whim of the different masters without special communication and assent. No object whatever can be more important, either with a view to the establishment or to the maintenance of every proper regulation, and faithful discharge of duty, than a certainty and frequency of impartial visitation and inspection. The general superintending power of government must encourage and enforce the full execution of every trust in every department. I think it right to declare that this plan is not of course designed to interfere with the progress of many schools already established, or to preclude the institution of others at the will of liberal individuals, who may be disposed to form them; but in many instances afford an example, worthy of imitation both in the modes of instruction, the rules of discipline, and the care of inspection.

After having proposed to you, for the reasons which I have assigned, the application of this system to all ranks of the community, let me indulge a hope, that my sentiments accord with the disposition of the committee, by recommending a participation of its benefits in general to our fellow-subjects of all religious persuasions, which are tolerated among us. When we reflect, that it is our great object to clear away the mists of ignorance, and to enlighten the understanding for the noblest purposes, of which man is capable by the improved endowments of his mind, let us not exclude from the means of a similar illumination, any description of the people who, by wandering in darkness and ignorance, stumble against the laws, causing confusion and disorder in the state, and pulling down disaster and ruin upon their own heads. There can be here, I conceive, no question of political reserve in such a case, whilst every principle of liberality and general fraternity should lead us to a different conclusion. We should not do justice to our own conviction of the superiority of our doctrines, if we retained any dread of raising or improving in those of a contrary communion a capacity to form a just comparison between them. It may, however, be proper that the instructors of the youth should be indispensably of the established religion, and that in some special cases education and support, where they are to be united at the charge of the state, should be confined, as they now are, to children brought up in the tenets of our own church. But in mentioning the probable expediency of this precaution, let me not on the other hand be misunderstood to force the obligations upon other sects to seek their only means of education under our preceptors. Let our schools be accessible to them, but make not their attendance thither compulsory. Hold out to them, as an invitation in general, the excellence of the opportunity, and let the inducement to acceptance be that of security against interference with their religious principles. The legislature thinks it wise and necessary to make distinctions for political purposes or purposes of state, but we need make none in the public facility of imbibing instruction with the general principles of morality, industry, truth, honesty and decorum, which it must be the interest, and indeed a part of the policy also of every well-regulated state, to disseminate and cherish as much as possible among all the component parts of its society.

The first object ... which presents it self to notice, in surveying the different divisions of this system, is the scheme by which the lowest and most numerous order of the community have within their reach such moderate advantages of instruction and precept as may make them at once more happy and more useful members of society. This object has in some degree already heretofore engaged the attention of the legislature by an act, which is still in force and observance, although the provisions of it do not go to form a sufficient establishment in these days; nor is the nature of the obligation under it such as in itself to secure the gratuitous communication of instruction to the poor, which I would which I wish to recommend in the strongest manner. If we look back for a moment to the history of the times, in which the act alluded to (28 Henry VIII, c. 15) was made, and consider the real motives of it, we shall find that there was something of policy as well as charity in the institution of parish schools under that reign; a policy, however, of most excellent tendency, and worthy of being perpetuated. The more general knowledge and use of the English language were certainly then, if not the sole, at least the principal objects of parliamentary concern, in directing the introduction of these schools; and it is to be further observed, that although the minister of the parish was obliged to teach such children as presented themselves, or to substitute a proper instructor, allowance was given to take a certain small stipend from the scholars for their tuition.

When I mention the English language to have been the only object of instruction in these schools, I do not mean to represent them in a more humble point of view on that account; but it will, on the contrary, be recollected, that great pains and also skill must have been required of a master who was capable of teaching, in effect, the knowledge and use of a dead language; for it was at that time as much unknown to the people as those of the antients [sic]. And therefore we should form an inadequate idea of those institutions, if we compared them immediately with our present notion or acquaintance of parish schools, wherein that which is called reading English is, I fear, little more than the articulation of certain sounds perfectly unincumbered with any regard to meaning. Whatever might have been either the object of instruction, or the execution of it in those days, and however competent the provision might then have been for the purpose, it is certain that neither the plan or the provision are efficient at present. Many reasons, which it is not necessary to enumerate, have probably by degrees contributed to the failure, and at last to the almost total disregard of these establishments. I do not mean to insinuate that the parochial minister, who, by his oath of induction and institution to his living, is bound to keep a school, or cause it to be kept in his parish, does not perform his compact in the usual way, which is by an allowance of 40s to the master, who with that encouragement is generally turned among the parishioners to try his chance of obtaining a livelihood by getting scholars.

Source: Extracts from Mr Orde's Plan of an Improved system of education in Ireland; submitted to the House of Commons, 12 April 1787; with the Debate which arose thereon. Reported by John Giffard, Esq., pp. 24–28; 30–33.

Speech reproduced by HardPress, Miami, 2019.

Bibliography

Primary Sources

Government Publications

7 William III, c. 4, 1695, *An Act to Restrain Foreign Education.*

9 William III, c. 1, 1697, *An Act for banishing all Papists exercising any Ecclesiastical Jurisdiction, and all Regulars of the Popish Clergy out of the Kingdom.*

12 Elizabeth I, c. 1, 1570, *An Act for the Erection of Free Schools.*

28 Henry VIII, c. 15, 1537, *An Act for the English Orde, Habite and Language.*

39/40 George III, c. 67, 1800, *The Union with Ireland Act.*

40 George III, c. 38, 1800, *The Act of Union (Ireland).*

A Bill Effectuating the Intercourse and Commerce Between Great Britain and Ireland, on Permanent and Equitable principles, for the Mutual Benefit of Both Kingdoms: Moved for in the House of Commons Ireland by the Right Hon. Thomas Orde, on Friday, August 12 1785, and presented by him on Monday, August 15. Author unknown.

First Report of the Commissioners of Irish Education Inquiry, H.C. 1825 (400).

A humble proposal for obtaining his majesty's royal charter to incorporate a society for promoting Christian knowledge among the poor natives of the kingdom of Ireland (1730). Quoted in M. G. Jones, *The charity school movement, a study of eighteenth-century puritanism in action* (London: 1964), 223–228. More recently: Cambridge University Press, 2013.

Journals of the House of Commons of the Kingdom of Ireland. Report of Her Majesty's Commissioners appointed to enquire into the endowments, funds and actual condition of all schools endowed for the purpose of education in Ireland, H.C. 1857-8 (2336-III).

Manuscripts

Bolton Manuscripts, National Manuscripts Library, National Library of Ireland, Kildare Street, Dublin.

Donoughmore Mss., 1891 – Published by the Historical manuscripts Commission; Trinity College, Dublin. From John Hely-Hutchinson, Provost of TCD, 1774–1794, and his son, the first Earl of Donoughmore, T/3459. Bolton Manuscripts, National Manuscripts Library, National Library of Ireland, Kildare Street, Dublin.

Ms. 15,884: Outline of a plan for a great school connected with the University, and some thoughts on school education in Ireland, by John Hely-Hutchinson.
Ms. 15,885: Observations by Thomas Orde on John Hely-Hutchinson's plan for a great school connected with the University, 1785.
Ms. 15,886(2): A Plan of Education – abstract Collegiate School, by Thomas Orde.
Ms. 15,881: Letters from the Bishops of Meath, Clogher, Waterford and Ossory, the Archbishop of Cashel, Sir Jeremiah Fitzpatrick and Mr John Ferrar, regarding the returns of Free schools of Royal Foundation, Orde's plan, the returns of Charter Schools, 1785–1787.
Ms. 15,882: Letters from Mr E. Tighe to Thomas Orde concerning the question of education.
Ms. 15,883: Letters to Thomas Orde from B. Roberts, E. Tighe, W. Cole, J. Reeves, John Fitzgibbon, Dr Allott, Bishop of Elphin, Archbishop Robinson, C. Agar and J. Giffard.
Ms. 15,886: Supplemental Observations on the Plan of Education, by John Hely-Hutchinson.
Ms. 15,887(1–10): Notes on Charter Schools, Erasmus Smith Schools, Blue Coat Hospital, Portarlington and Ballyroan Schools, Diocesan Schools. Ideas on a second university and memo to John Hely-Hutchinson, by Thomas Orde.
Ms. 15,888: Mr Orde's Plan of an improved system of education in Ireland: Submitted to the House of Commons. 12 April 1787, with the debate which arose thereon, 1787. John Giffard, Dublin, 1787.
Ms. 16,354: Communications from Charles Dodgson, Bishop of Elphin and John Hely-Hutchinson.
Ms. 16,360: Plan of Education for Ireland. Thomas Orde.
Ms. 16,369: And memoranda, including education. By Thomas Orde.
Ms. 16,372: System of Education, College of Visitors and Inspectors. By Thomas Orde.

Secondary Sources

Books

Akenson, Donald Harman, *The Irish Education Experiment: The National System of Education in the Nineteenth Century* (London: Routledge and Kegan Paul, 1970).
Analecta Hibernica, No. 1, March 1930.
Archer, M. S., *Social Origins of Educational Systems* (London: Routledge, 2013).
Archer, Margaret Scotford, *Social Origins of Educational Systems* (London: Sage Publications, 1979).
Armytage, W. H. G., *Four Hundred Years of English Education* (Cambridge: Cambridge University Press, 1965).

Aston, N. and Campbell Orr, C. eds, *An Enlightenment Statesman in Whig Britain: Lord Shelburne in Context, 1737–1805* (Woodbridge: Boydell Press, 2011).

Atkinson, Norman, *Irish Education: A History of Educational Institutions* (Dublin: Allen Figgis, 1969).

Auchmuty, James Johnston, *Irish Education: A History of Educational Institutions* (Dublin: Hodges Figgis, 1937). Pub. Online by Cambridge University Press, 2016.

Balfour, Graham, *The Education Systems of Great Britain and Ireland* (Oxford: Clarendon Press, 1903).

Bardon, Bardon, *A History of Ireland in 250 Episodes* (Dublin: Gill and Macmillan, 2009).

Barnard, H. C., *A History of English Education from 1760* (London: University of London Press, 1966), 45.

Ohlmeyer, Bartlett T., and Smith, Kelly J., eds, *The Cambridge History of Ireland* (Cambridge: Cambridge University Press, 2020). Chapter by James Kelly, 'The Politics of Protestant Ascendancy 1730–1790', in vol. 3.

Bartlett, Thomas, *The Fall and Rise of the Irish Nation: The Catholic Question, 1690–1830* (Dublin: Gill and Macmillan, 1992).

Batterbury, R., *Oideachas in Éirinn, 1500–1946* (Dublin: Stationery Office, 1955).

Beames, Michael, *Peasants and Power: The Whiteboy Movements and Their Control in Pre-Famine Ireland* (Sussex: The harvester Press, 1983).

Beckett, J. C., *A Short History of Ireland* (London: Hutchinson University Library, 1973).

Beckett, J. C., *The Making of Modern Ireland, 1603–1923* (London: Faber and Faber, 1981).

Bergin, J., Magennis, E., Ní Mhunghaile, L., and Walsh, P., eds, 'New Perspectives on the Penal Laws', *Eighteenth-Century Ireland/Special Issue* (2011).

Boaden, J., ed., *The Private Correspondence of David Garrick: With the Most Celebrated Persons of His Time* (Cambridge: Cambridge University Press 2013), ii.

Brady, Ciarán, ed., *Ideology and the Historians* (Dublin: Lilliput Press, 1991).

Brennan, C., *A Critical Review of the Bishop of Cloyne's Publication; with Occasional Remarks on the Production of Some Other Writers, Particularly Those of Trinity College, and on the Conduct of the Present Ministry. Addressed to His Lordship, by an Unbiassed Irishman – pseud. for Charles Brennan* (Dublin: Printed by John Chambers, 1787). Electronic version, Farmington Hills, Michigan: Thomson Gale, 2003).

Burke, Edmund (ed. Matthew Arnold), *Irish Affairs* (London: The Cresset Library, 1881).

Byrne F. J., Vaughan, W. E., Cosgrove, A., Hill, J. R., and Ó Cróinín, D., eds, *A New History of Ireland: Eighteenth-Century Ireland, 1691–1800,* vol. IV (Oxford: Oxford University Press, 2009).

Canny, N., *Kingdom and Colony: Ireland in the Atlantic World, 1560–1800* (Baltimore, 1988).

Chauviré, Roger, *History of Ireland* (Dublin: Clonmore and Reynolds, 1956), 92. Translated by the Earl of Wicklow.

Cokayne, G. E., *The Complete Peerage,* vol. 2 (London: Franklin Classics, 2018).

Connolly, S. J., ed., *Political Ideas in Eighteenth-Century Ireland* (Dublin: Four Courts Press, 2000).

Coolahan, John, *Irish Education: History and Structure* (Dublin: Institute of Public Administration, 1981).

Coolahan, John, *Towards the Era of Lifelong Learning: A History of Irish Education, 1800–2016* (Dublin: Institute of Public Administration, 2017).

Corcoran, T., *State Policy in Irish Education A.D. 1536–1816* (Dublin: Fallon Brothers, 1916).

Cullen, L. M., ed., *The Formation of the Irish Economy* (Cork: Mercier Press, 1979).

Curtis, Edmund, *A History of Ireland* (London: Methuen, 1961).

Curtis, S. J., *History of Education in Great Britain* (London: University Tutorial Press, 1950).

Dickinson, Harry T., *Ireland in the Age of Revolution, 1760–1805,* vol. 3 (London: Pickering and Chatto, 2013).

Donnelly, James S. Jr., and Miller, K. A., eds, *Irish Popular Culture 1650–1850* (Dublin: Irish Academic Press, 1999).

Dowling, P. J., *A History of Irish Education* (Cork: Mercier Press, 1971).

Doyle, Joseph, *Model Schools – Model Teachers? A Nineteenth-Century Irish Teacher-Training Initiative* (Kilkenny: Geata Buidhe Books, 2020).

Duke, John, ed., *Correspondence between the Right Honble; William Pitt and Charles Duke of Rutland, Lord Lieutenant of Ireland, 1781–1787* (London: William Blackwood and Sons, 1890; reprint: Forgotten Books, 2015).

Edgeworth, R. L., *Essays on Professional Education* (London: Johnston and Co., 1809), 40–41. Republished Cambridge University Press, 2013.

Curtis Edmund, *A History of Ireland* (London: Methuen, 1961), 296.

Tighe Edward (Melantius), *A Letter Addressed to Mr. Orde, upon the Education of the People* (Dublin: Printed by P. Byrne, 1787).

Fagan, Patrick, *Divided Loyalties: The Question of an Oath for Irish Catholics in the Eighteenth Century* (Dublin: Four Courts Press, 1997).

Farrell Brian, ed., *The Irish Parliamentary Tradition* (Dublin: Gill and Macmillan, 1973).

Field J., *The Life of John Howard with Comments on His Character and Philanthropic Labours* (London: Longman, Brown, Green Longmans, 1850), 142. See Facsilime: Published by Fb&c Limited, 2018.

Finn, Rex Welldon, *Introducing Ireland* (London: Museum Press, 1955).

Fitzgerald, G., *Irish Primary Education in the Early Nineteenth Century: An Analysis of the First and Second Reports of the Commissioners of Irish Education Inquiry, 1825–1826* (Dublin: Royal Irish Academy, 2013).

Fitzpatrick, J., *An Essay on Gaol-Abuses, and on the Means of Redressing Them: Together with the General Method of Treating Disorders to Which Prisoners Are Most Incident* (Dublin: Byrne and Brown, 1784).

Fleming, N. C., 'Education since the Late Eighteenth Century', in Liam Kennedy and Philip Ollerenshaw, eds, *Ulster since 1600: Politics, Economy, and Society* (Oxford: Oxford University Press, 2013).

Foster, R. F., *Modern Ireland, 1600–1972* (London: Penguin Books, 1989).

Fourteenth Report of the Commissioners of the Board of Education in Ireland, H.C. 1812/13 (21) vi, 221.

Froude, J. A., *The English in Ireland in the Eighteenth Century*, vol. II (London: Longmans, 1881).

Giffard, J., *Mr. Orde's Plan of an Improved System of Education in Ireland; Submitted to the House of Commons, 12 April 1787; with the Debate Which Arose Thereon* (Dublin: Publisher/Printer, W. Porter, 1787), 140. Republished as facsimile edition by Hard Press, Miami, 2019.

Giffard, John, *Mr. Orde's Plan of an Improved System of Education in Ireland: Submitted to the House of Commons, 12 April 1787; with the Debate Which Arose Thereon* (Dublin: Printed by W. Porter, 1787; reprint: Miami: Hard Press, 2019).

Godkin, James, *A Hand-Book of the Education Question: Education in Ireland; Its History, Institutions, Systems, Statistics, and Progress, from the Earliest Times to the Present* (Dublin: Printed by Alexander Thom, 1862).

Green, Andy, *Education and State Formation: The Rise of Education Systems in England, France and the USA* (London: Macmillan, 1990).

Hamilton, Elizabeth, *Cottagers of Glenburnie* (Palala Press, 2015, 1st edn 1808).

Hans, Nicholas, *New Trends in Education in the Eighteenth Century* (London: Routledge and Kegan Paul, 1966).

Haugaard, Mark, and Ryan, Kevin, 'Power and Powerlessness', in Sara O'Sullivan, ed., *Contemporary Ireland: A Sociological Map* (Dublin: University College Press, 2007).

Hayden, Mary, and Moonan, G. A., eds, *A Short History of the Irish People; from 1603 to 1924* (Dublin: Talbot Press, 1921).

Hayton, D. W., and Bartlett, T. eds, *Penal Era and Golden Age: Essays in Irish History, 1690–1800* Belfast: Ulster Historical Foundation, 1979).

Hayton, D. W., *The Anglo-Irish Experience, 1680–1730: Religion, Identity and Patriotism* (Woodbridge: Boydell Press, 2012).

Higgins, Pádhraig, *A Nation of Politicians: Gender, Patriotism, and Political Culture in Late Eighteenth-Century Ireland* (Wisconsin: University of Wisconsin Press, 2010).

Horn, Pamela, *Education in Rural England, 1800–1914* (Dublin: Gill and Macmillan, 1978).

Howard, D. L., *John Howard: Prisoner Reformer* (London: Johnson, 1958).

Hyland, Áine, and Milne, Kenneth, eds, *Irish Educational Documents,* vol. 1 (Dublin: Church of Ireland College of Education, 1987).

An Inquiry into Some of the Causes of the Ill Situation of the Affairs of Ireland (Dublin, 1731); *Considerations on Several Proposals for Preventing the Exportation of Wool* ... (London, 1741).

Jarman, T. L., *Landmarks in the History of Education* (London: John Murray, 1963).

Johnston, Edith Mary, *Ireland in the Eighteenth Century.* Gill History of Ireland Series (Dublin: Gill and Macmillan, 1974).

Jones, M. G., *The Charity School Movement: A Study of Eighteenth-Century Puritanism in Action* (London: Frank Cass, 1964).

Journals of the House of Commons of the Kingdom of Ireland. Report of Her Majesty's Commissioners Appointed to Enquire into the Endowments, Funds and Actual Condition of All Schools Endowed for the Purpose of Education in Ireland, H.C. 1857-8 (2336-111).

Kelly, James, and Hegarty, Susan, eds, Schools and Schooling, 1650-2000: New Perspectives on the History of Education (Dublin: Four Courts Press, 2017).

Kelly, James, *Dictionary of Irish Biography* (2009).

Kelly, James, *Prelude to Union: Anglo-Irish Politics in the 1780s* (Cork: Cork University Press, 1992).

Keogh, Dáire, *The French Disease: The Catholic Church and Irish Radicalism, 1790-1800* (Dublin: Four Courts Press, 1993).

Lawrence, Elizabeth, *The Origins and Growth of Modern Education* (London: Penguin, 1970).

Lawson, John, and Silver, Harold, *A Social History of Education in England* (London: Routledge, 1973; e-book, 2013).

Lecky, W. E. H., *A History of Ireland in the Eighteenth Century* (London: Longmans, 1902).

Lecky, W. E. H., *A History of Ireland in the Eighteenth Century,* 8 vols (London: Longmans, Green and Co., 1913).

Leighton, C. D. A., *Catholicism in a Protestant Kingdom: A Study of the Irish Ancien Régime* (Dublin: Gill and MacMillan, 1994).

Locker Lampson, G., *A Consideration of the State of Ireland in the Nineteenth Century* (London: A. Constable, 1907), 125.
Lord Mountmorres, *The Crisis: A Collection of Essays Written in the Years 1792 and 1793, upon Toleration, Public Credit, and Other Interesting Subjects* (London: Hookham and Carpenter, 1794).
Lougheed, Kevin, 'National Education and Empire: Ireland and the Geography of the National Education System', in David Dickson, Justyna Pyz, and Christopher Shepard, eds, *Irish Classrooms and British Empire: Imperial Contexts in the Origins of Modern Education* (Dublin: Four Courts Press, 2012).
Lyons, Tony, *The Education Work of Richard Lovell Edgeworth, Irish Educator and Inventor, 1744-1817* (Lewiston: Mellen Press, 2003).
Lyons, Tony, The Pay Schools of Ireland and their Interface with the National System of Education (Oxford: Peter Lang, 2023).
MacCurtain, Margaret, Tudor and Stuart Ireland (Dublin: Gill and McMillan, 1972).
MacDonagh, Oliver, *The Inspector General: Sir Jeremiah Fitzpatrick and Social Reform, 1783-1802* (London: Croom Helm, 1981).
Mack, Edward, *Public Schools and Public Opinion 1780-1860: An Examination of the Relationship between Contemporary Ideas and the Evolution of an English Institution* (London: Methuen, 1938).
Máire and Conor Cruise O'Brien, *Ireland: A Concise History* (London: BCA, 1992).
Malcomson, A. P. W., *Archbishop Charles Agar: Churchmanship and Politics in Ireland, 1760 -1810* (Dublin: Four Courts Press, 2002).
Malcomson, A. P. W., *John Foster: The Politics of the Anglo-Irish Ascendancy* (Oxford: Oxford University Press, 1978).
Mansergh, Danny, *Grattan's Failure: Parliamentary Opposition and the People in Ireland, 1779 -1800* (Dublin: Irish Academic Press, 2005).
Mansergh, Martin, *The Legacy of History* (Cork: Mercier Press, 2003).
McBride, Ian, *Eighteenth-Century Ireland: The Isle of Slaves* (Dublin: Gill and Macmillan, 2009).
McCracken, J. L., *The Irish Parliament in the Eighteenth Century* (Dundalk: Dundalgan Press, 1971).
McDowell, R. B., *Ireland in the Age of Imperialism and Revolution, 1760-1801* (Oxford: Clarendon Press, 1979).
McDowell, R. B., *Irish Public Opinion, 1750-1800* (Connecticut: Greenwood Press, 1975).
McGuire, J., and Milne, K., eds, *As by Law Established: The Church of Ireland since the Reformation* (Dublin: The Lilliput Press, 1995). Pub. Online by Cambridge University Press, 2009.
McManus, Antonia, *The Irish Hedge School and Its Books, 1695-1831* (Dublin: Four Courts Press, 2002).

McNally, Patrick, *Parties, Patriots and Undertakers: Parliamentary Politics in Early Hanoverian Ireland* (Dublin: Four Courts Press, 1997).

Mill, James, 'Education', in *Supplement to the Encyclopaedia Britanica* (London, 1819), 18-19.

Milne, Kenneth, *The Irish Charter Schools, 1730-1830* (Dublin: Four Courts Press, 1997).

Moody, T. W., and Martin, F. X., eds, *The Course of Irish History* (Cork: Mercier Press, 1994).

Moody, T. W., and Vaughan, W. E., *A New History of Ireland, vol. IV. Eighteenth-Century Ireland, 1691-1800* (Oxford: Oxford University Press, 1985).

Morley, Vincent, *The Popular Mind in Eighteenth-Century Ireland* (Cork: Cork University Press, 2017).

Morton, Grenfell, *Elizabethan Ireland* (London: Longman, 1971).

O'Brien, Gerard, *Anglo-Irish Politics in the Age of Grattan and Pitt* (Dublin: Irish Academic Press, 1987).

O'Brien, Gerard, ed., *Catholic Ireland in the Eighteenth Century: Collected Essays of Maureen Wall* (Dublin: Geography Publications, 1989).

O'Brien, Gerard, ed., *Parliament, Politics and People: Essays in Eighteenth-Century Irish History* (Dublin: Irish Academic Press, 1989).

O'Brien, Gerard, *Parliament, Politics and People: Essays in Eighteenth-Century Irish History* (Dublin: Irish Academic Press, 1989).

O'Brien, Máire, and O'Brien, Conor Cruise, *Ireland: A Concise History* (London: BCA, 1992).

O'Riordan, Michael, *Catholicity and Progress* (London: K. Paul, Trench, Trubner and Co., 1906).

O'Sullivan, T., 'Between Toleration and Preservation: The Popery Laws and Irish Anglicanism, 1782-1808', in *New Perspectives on the Penal Laws* (Dublin: Eighteenth-Century Ireland, Special Issue, no. 1, 2011).

Orde-Powlett, Thomas, *Mr. Orde's Plan of an Improved System of Education in Ireland* (Speech in the Irish House of Commons, College Green, Dublin, 1787; Reprint: United States of America, Nabu Press, n.d.).

Owen, J. B., *The Eighteenth Century 1714-1815* (London: Nelson, 1974).

Palmer, Stanley H., *Police and Protest in England and Ireland, 1780 -1850* (Cambridge: Cambridge University Press, 1990).

Parkes, Susan, *A Guide to Sources for the History of Irish Education, 1780-1922* (Dublin: Four Courts Press, 2010).

Plumb, J. H., *England in the Eighteenth Century* (London: Penguin Books, 1980).

Powell, Martyn J., *Britain and Ireland in the Eighteenth-Century Crisis of Empire* (Basingstoke: Palgrave Macmillan, 2003).

Power, T. P., and Whelan, Kevin, eds, *Endurance and Emergence: Catholics in Ireland in the Eighteenth Century* (Dublin: Irish Academic Press, 1990).

Raftery, Deirdre, and Fischer, Karin, eds, *Educating Ireland: Schooling and Social Change, 1700-2000* (Dublin: Irish Academic Press, 2014).

Raftery, Deirdre, and Parkes, Susan, *Female Education in Ireland 1700-1900: Minerva or Madonna* (Dublin: Irish Academic Press, 2007).

Reeves, Marjorie, *Female Education and Nonconformist Culture, 1700-1900* (London: Leicester University Press, 1997).

Ross, G., ed., *The Correspondence of Charles, First Marquess Cornwallis*, vol. 1 (London: J. Murray, 1859).

Rousseau, Jean-Jacques, *Emile; or on Education* (Penguin Classics, 1991).

Sanderson, Michael, *Education, Economic Change and Society in England 1780-1870* (London: The McMillan Press, 1983).

Silver, Harold, *English Education and the Radicals, 1780 -1850* (London: Routledge and Kegan Paul, 1975).

Smith, Adam, *The Wealth of Nations*, 2 vols (London, 1776).

Smyth, J., *Men of No Property: Irish Radicals and Popular Politics in the Late Eighteenth Century* (Dublin: Gill and Macmillan, 1992).

St. Brendan's Church of Ireland, Tarbert 1814-2014: 200 Years of Change (Tarbert Historical and Heritage Society, 2014).

Taylor, John, *Amalgamation of Unions, and Pauper and National Education in Ireland* (Dublin: John Falconer, 1857).

The Life of John Howard, Esquire: The Philanthropist (Edinburgh, 1825; Anonymous). Reprinted by Palala Press, USA, 2015).

The Manuscripts and Correspondence of James, First Earl of Charlemont, vol. 2, 1784-1799, pt. 4 (London: Eyre and Spottiswoode, 1894).

Thomson, D., *England in The Nineteenth Century* (London: Penguin, 1970).

Tighe, Robert Stearne, *Melantius, a Letter Addressed to Mr. Orde upon the Education of the People* (Dublin: Printed by P. Byrne, 1787; Reprint: Nabu Press, 2011).

Todd, Janet, *Mary Wollstonecraft: A Revolutionary Life* (London: Phoenix Press).

Troy, John T., *The Excommunication of the Rev. Robert McEvoy, Priest of the Dublin Archdiocese for Promulgating and Upholding Principles Established by the French Revolution* (London: Printed by J. P. Coghlan, 1798).

Uglow, Jenny, *The Lunar Men: The Friends Who Made the Future, 1730-1810* (London: Faber and Faber, 1988).

Venn, J. A., *Alumni Cantabrigienses* (a biographical history of all known students, graduates and holders of office at the University of Cambridge, from the earliest times to 1900) (Cambridge: Cambridge University Press, 1951).

Venn, J. A., *Alumni Cantabrigienses,* pt. 2, vol. 4. Kahlenberg-Oyler (Cambridge: Cambridge University Press, 1951). Republished by CUP in 2012.

Walsh, Brendan, ed., *Education Studies in Ireland: Key Disciplines* (Dublin: Gill and Macmillan, 2011).

Ward, Robert E., *An Encyclopedia of Irish Schools, 1500-1800* (Lewiston: Edwin Mellen Press, 1995).

Wardle, David, *English Popular Education, 1780-1970* (Cambridge: Cambridge University Press, 1970).

Woods, C. J., ed., *Journals & Memoirs of Thomas Russell* (Dublin: Irish Academic Press, 1991).

York, Neil Longley, *Neither Kingdom Nor Nation: The Irish Quest for Constitutional Rights, 1698-1800* (Washington, DC: The Catholic University of America Press, 1994).

Journals/Articles/Theses

Bartlett, Thomas, 'The Rise and Fall of the Protestant Nation, 1690-1800', *Éire-Ireland* Summer (1991), 7- 18.

Beckett, J. C., 'The Irish Parliament in the Eighteenth Century', *Natural History Society Procedures* 4 (1950–1955), 17–37.

Burns, R. E., 'The Irish Popery Laws: A Study of Eighteenth-Century Legislation and Behaviour', *Review of Politics* 21 (1959), 276–279.

Burton, Edward F., 'Richard Lovell Edgeworth's Education Bill of 1799: A Missing Chapter in the History of Irish Education', *The Irish Journal of Education* xiii/ 1 (1979), 24–33, 25.

Corcoran, T., 'The Dublin Education Bill of 1787', *The Irish Monthly* 59/ 698 (1931), 495–500.

Dublin Evening Post (April 13 and 19, August 28, September 8 and 20), 1787.

Helena Kelleher Hahn, '"Objects of Raging Detestation": The Charter Schools', *History Ireland* 19/ 2 (2011), 24–27.

Jacques, William, *The Chief Factors Determining the Developments in Primary Education, Ireland, 1831–1947* (Unpublished Doctoral Thesis, Queen's University, Belfast, 1952), ch. 1.

Kellehan-Kahn, H., '"Objects of Raging Detestation": The Charter Schools', *History Ireland* 19/2 (2011), 24.

Kelly, James, 'The Context and Course of Thomas Orde's Plan of Education of 1787', *The Irish Journal of Education* 20/1 (1986), 3–26.

Lougheed, Kevin, *National Education and the State: An Historical Geography of the Emergence of National Education in Pre-Famine Ireland* (Doctoral Thesis submitted to the School of Natural Science, the University of Dublin, Trinity College, 2014).

Lyons, Tony, 'Hedge Schools of Kerry', *Journal of the Kerry Archaeological and Historical Society* 2/4 (2004), 133–152.
McElroy, Colm, 'Thomas Orde and Educational Innovation, 1786–1787', *Irish Educational Studies* 15 (1996), 152–163.
McElroy, Colm, *Thomas Orde, 1746–1807: Educational Innovator* (M.Ed., Thesis submitted to University College Dublin, 1994).
Milne, Kenneth, 'Irish Charter Schools', *The Irish Journal of Education* 8/1 (1974), 3–29.
Milne, Kenneth, 'The Irish Charter Schools: The Grand Design in Principle and Practice', *Irish Educational Studies* 4/1 (1984), 35–53.
O'Higgins, Laurie, '(In)Felix Paupertas: Scholarship of the Eighteenth-Century Irish Poor', *Arethusa* 40/3 (2007), 421–450.
Parkes, Susan, 'Irish education in the British Parliamentary Papers, 1801–1922', *History of Education Society* (1978).
Parliamentary Register of the Irish House of Commons, vols 6 and 7 (1787).
Quane, Michael, 'The Diocesan Schools – 1570–1870', *Journal of the Cork Historical and Archaeological Society* (Jan. – June 1961), 26–49.
Report of the Commissioners of Irish Education Enquiry (1791), in *Report of the Commissioners Appointed to Inquire into the Endowments, Funds and Actual Conditions of All Schools Endowed for the Purpose of Education in Ireland,* vol. II, H.C. 1857-8 (2336-I) XXII, pt. III. Reprinted by Hard Press, Miami, 2019.
Sullivan, J. J. *The Education of Irish Catholics, 1782–1831* (Doctoral Thesis submitted to Queen's University, Belfast, 1959).
Taylor, Brian W., 'Jeremy Bentham and the Education of the Irish People', *The Irish Journal of Education* 14/1 (1980), 19–32.
Tikly, Leon, 'Governmentality and the Study of Education Policy in South Africa', *Journal of Education Policy* 18/2 (2003), 162–165.
Volunteer Evening Post, Dublin: Jan. 2 – Dec. 29, 1787.

Index

www.ingramcontent.com/pod-product-compliance
Ingram Content Group UK Ltd.
Pitfield, Milton Keynes, MK11 3LW, UK
UKHW021825120926
8556IPUK00043B/1040

9 781803 743516